From shodo—"the Way of calligraphy"—to budo—"the martial Way"—the Japanese have succeeded in designing their traditional arts and crafts as paths to meditation. The names of these skills frequently end with the word Do, also pronounced Michi, which equals the "Way." When practicing a Way, we unearth universal principles that go beyond a specific discipline, relating to the art of living itself. Featuring the books of H. E. Davey and other select writers, works by **Michi Publishing** center on these Do forms. Michi Publishing's focus is on classical Asian arts, spirituality, and meditation, benefiting all cultures.

SHIN-SHIN-TOITSU: *"unification of mind and body,"* painted in
the style of Kobara Ranseki Sensei. Calligraphy by H. E. Davey.

JAPANESE YOGA

The Way of

Dynamic

Meditation

H. E. Davey

Michi Publishing • Albany, California

NOTE TO READERS

Shin-shin-toitsu-do, or Japanese yoga, involves the movement of both mind and body. As with any method of physical training or psychological practice, if the techniques depicted in this book are misused, misinterpreted, or incorrectly practiced, injuries and other problems may result. The author and publisher will not be held responsible in any manner for any injuries or damage of any kind that may occur as the result of following the directions presented in this book. No claims regarding the suitability of any of the techniques described or illustrated in this book for the treatment of any physical or psychological disorder are made or should be inferred. Readers are encouraged to seek appropriate medical and psychological advice before undertaking the practice of Japanese yoga or any of the procedures presented in this book. Readers are also advised to practice the methods outlined in this book only under the direct guidance of a qualified instructor.

Published by Michi Publishing
michipublishing@yahoo.com

All photography and portrait of Nakamura Tempu Sensei on page 7 by Steve Aibel.

All calligraphy by the author.

Cover design by Linda Ronan based on a concept by Steve Aibel; the calligraphy by H. E. Davey is an abstract version of the character *shin* (the first character in Shin-shin-toitsu-do), meaning "mind."

Printed in the United States of America.

CONTENTS

NAKAMURA TEMPU SENSEI (1876–1968)
Illustration by Steve Aibel

PREFACE

I hesitated to write a book about the Shin-shin-toitsu-do system of Japanese yoga for many years. It's not because I feel unqualified to write such a work, although I certainly have not completely mastered any of the exercises in this book.

No author is ever truly qualified to write about any of the Japanese Arts and Ways. Complete mastery of such profound disciplines isn't really possible. Nevertheless, if everyone with experience in a "Do" ("Way") like *shodo*, Japanese calligraphy, or *kado*, Japanese flower arrangement, waited until he or she was ready to write the perfect volume, no books would ever appear.

I teach Shin-shin-toitsu-do full-time at the Sennin Foundation Center for Japanese Cultural Arts. I've written about Japanese healing arts, martial arts, and fine arts for various periodicals over the years, even writing (with Hashimoto Tetsuichi Sensei) the first English-language magazine article about the founder of Shin-shin-toitsu-do. I'm the author of three books on three different Japanese cultural arts, and still I wavered when it came to this book. Why?

FROM THE UNIVERSAL TO THE PARTICULAR

My faltering was due to several reasons, and the examination of these reasons will perhaps shed light on the nature of both myself and the art of Japanese yoga. First, most Japanese Do forms involve examining ourselves in great detail through the penetrating study of a single art. From the in-depth examination of this particular art, students may discover principles relating to all aspects of life—from the particular to the universal.

But Shin-shin-toitsu-do, in its ultimate sense, represents something different from these other Ways. It's not actually the study of various stretching exercises and forms of meditation as many believe, but rather, it is the direct investigation of universal principles for living— from the universal to the particular. By understanding these principles, various particular aspects of our lives are forever transformed. This is obviously valuable, but unless it's correctly approached, the direct study of universal principles can be excessively vague and abstract, eventually degenerating into meaningless philosophical discourse or "mind candy," if you will.

It is especially difficult to avoid this tendency when writing a book about such universal principles, and it can even be troublesome when practicing face-to-face with friends. Yet like many things in life, the simplest way to avoid a problem is to acknowledge the potential for difficulty and face it squarely. Hopefully this is what we'll be doing throughout *Japanese Yoga: The Way of Dynamic Meditation*.

AN IMMEDIATE AND PERSONAL EXPERIENCING OF THE WAY

Second, because trying to look directly at the principles underlying everything—the Way of the universe—can become pretty abstract and is usually arduous, people have a strong inclination to simply memorize concepts they hear or read about. This propensity is markedly powerful when reading about matters of this nature, and yet, it is the absolute kiss of death (despite the fact that many "spiritual leaders" would encourage such rote learning).

Memorizing someone else's explanation of the truth isn't the same as seeing the truth for yourself. It is what it is—the memorization of secondhand knowledge. It is not your experience. It is not your knowledge. And no matter how much material is learned by rote, and no matter how eloquently we can speak about the memorized information, we're clinging to a description of something that's not ours. What's more, the description is never the item itself. By holding onto our impression of certain descriptions, we frequently are unable to see the real thing when it's right before our eyes. We are conditioned by memorizing and believing concepts—the truth of which we've never genuinely seen for ourselves.

When ongoing Shin-shin-toitsu-do training is conducted in a group, face-to-face, it is much easier to avoid this pitfall, but a book or a short public lecture is another matter altogether. For this reason, I decided to address this topic immediately in *Japanese Yoga*. Moreover, I've built a number of questions into the book for us to mutually consider, and in some cases I've deliberately made no attempt to answer these questions in print. Instead of offering pat answers, which is actually detrimental, I've tried to create a situation that will encourage us to jointly discover the truth of the universe for ourselves. Based on my above comments, which are repeated in varying forms throughout this work, I think you can see why I've adopted this approach.

I've also tried to make use of "experiments" to illustrate the principles of mind and body unification that make up Japanese yoga. By experimenting, the reader is encouraged to look seriously at himself or

PREFACE

herself and what's taking place at the moment. Through the use of such experiments, Nakamura Tempu Sensei, founder of Shin-shin-toitsu-do, hoped that students would be able to experience these principles firsthand, and thus gain genuine understanding of them.

LEARNING DIRECTLY FROM THE UNIVERSE

Finally, I've been very concerned that readers would see me as some sort of self-styled guru or spiritual authority. I absolutely reject this role. To look to another for the truth is to miss the Way of the universe that's eternally right before our eyes. It's to attempt to see through the eyes of another person, and it is destined to result in delusion—the follower believes he's seen the truth, but he's only seen a reflection of the truth at best, and the leader believes he or she is doing something right because of the worshipful attitude of the followers.

During his long life, Indian spiritual teacher Jiddhu Krishnamurti frequently and decisively commented on this phenomenon:

> If you would seek the Truth you must go out, far away
> from the limitations of the human mind and heart and
> there discover it—and that Truth is within yourself. Is it
> not much simpler to make Life itself the goal than to
> have mediators, gurus, who must inevitably step down
> the Truth and hence betray it?[1]

In some cases, the relationship between leaders and followers is innocent (but still harmful) mutual delusion. In other instances, it is exploitation. And in the end, the exploiter is exploited. Nevertheless, many will still choose to follow others, because to look for the truth always involves a leap into the complete unknown. To the best of my

11

knowledge, Nakamura Sensei did not tell students *what to do*. Instead, he offered them a means to discover *how to do it*. My purpose in writing this book is to share meaningful techniques of mind and body coordination with others, not to produce an exposition on what we should do with our lives—that is something each of us has to discover personally.

ABOUT THIS BOOK

I've learned a great deal by writing this book. (This is usually the case with my writing, and it's one of the reasons that I enjoy doing it.) It is my hope that both writer and reader can grow together mutually using this work as a catalyst. To help us do so, I've organized the text logically. I have started with this preface, proceeded to a brief history of Shin-shin-toitsu-do, and gone on to the basic principles of mind and body coordination that comprise the art. Be sure to read all of this before moving to the sections on meditation, health exercises, and healing arts. All of these various methods are based on a related set of universal principles. In my description of these principles, I've included some fun experiments, so don't mistakenly think that these chapters are merely dry, philosophical discourse. Chapter 9 deals with simple but profoundly challenging and valuable stretching exercises included in some versions of Shin-shin-toitsu-do. Finally, I've added a section with information about continuing your practice.

Since this book wasn't written with experts in mind, I've tried to avoid using complicated medical, anatomical, and psychological nomenclature. In doing so, I have used broad, general terminology, putting descriptions in laymen's terms whenever possible. At the same time, so as not to lose the cultural flavor of Shin-shin-toitsu-do, I've employed Japanese words to describe aspects of this Way that are so unique and distinctive that, in some cases, an exact English equivalent cannot be found. In other instances, I preferred to use Japanese words that the typical Western reader has little familiarity with—thus avoiding his or her possible assumptions and preconceived ideas. A glossary of these terms is provided at the end of the book.

Readers should realize that, while I've been careful about the words that I used and the phrases I selected for this book, all of its descriptions are approximations. By this I mean that the descriptions only point at a state beyond definition. Which is even more reason to find the truth directly rather than depend solely on the descriptions of others. At the same time, we should be careful about not reading whatever we want into what people say or write.

It was not possible for me to detail all the various methods taught in Shin-shin-toitsu-do. Shin-shin-toitsu-do is an extremely multifaceted art, and since the passing of Nakamura Tempu Sensei in the late 1960s his students have developed more than one version of it. I've studied both the original and modified versions of this art, and the material presented in my book reflects that fact. And like many books, *Japanese Yoga* bears more than a few traces of the person who wrote it. In plain English, this work is not the "official version" of anything (other than what my associates and I are presently experimenting with at the Sennin Foundation Center for Japanese Cultural Arts).

WHAT DO YOU MEAN BY "JAPANESE YOGA"?

People often phone the Sennin Foundation Center wondering about the difference between Japanese yoga and "regular yoga." By "regular yoga," they usually mean the original Indian yoga, and by Indian yoga, most callers actually mean Hatha yoga, which is the most widely practiced form of yoga in the West. Many readers may be wondering the same thing.

Hatha yoga is actually only one version of Indian yoga, and it specializes in the practice of stretching and yogic "postures," or *asana*. Pranayama breathing exercises are also sometimes included. In comparison to Hatha yoga, Shin-shin-toitsu-do is a more diverse Way, although the ultimate goal of both practices appears to be the same. Shin-shin-toitsu-do includes a wide variety of stretching exercises, breathing methods, forms of seated meditation and moving meditation, massage-like healing arts, techniques of auto-suggestion, and mind and body coordination drills, as well as principles for the unification of mind and body.

These principles of mind and body coordination are regarded as universal laws that express the workings of nature on human life. As such, they can be applied directly to an endless number of everyday activities and tasks. It is not uncommon when studying Japanese yoga to encounter classes and seminars that deal with the direct application of these universal principles to office work, sales, management, sports, art, music, public speaking, and a host of other topics. How to use these precepts of mind and body integration to realize our full potential in any action is the goal. All drills, exercises, and practices of Shin-shin-toitsu-do are based on the same principles, thus linking intelligently a diversity of arts. But more than this, they serve as vehicles for grasping and cultivating the principles of mind and body coordination. And it is these principles that can be put to use directly, unobtrusively, and immediately in our daily lives.

For example, while certain stretching methods and breathing techniques may be capable of enhancing relaxation, when we find ourselves losing composure in a business meeting we can't just drop to the floor to stretch or lead a discussion while performing deep breathing. But we can alter our posture and focus psychophysical energy in the lower abdomen pretty much anywhere and at any time. And this can result in not only coordination of mind and body—self-harmony in other words—but unshakeable calmness.

Shin-shin-toitsu-do includes such a wide variety of arts as a result of Nakamura Sensei's worldwide travels to find a cure for his tuberculosis. Mr. Nakamura studied different forms of yoga quite intensely in India, and this was the last stop on his global search. Prior to his study of yoga, he was deeply involved in Japanese spiritual methodologies and martial arts. He studied psychology in Europe. He obtained a medical degree in the United States. His explanations of yogic concepts and his teachings in general were greatly influenced by all these things. In many ways, Nakamura Sensei seems to have viewed his Japanese yoga as an integration of psychology and physical education that transcended both. While individual aspects of Shin-shin-toitsu-do can be found in other disciplines, as a whole the art comprises something distinctly unique unto itself.

Shin-shin-toitsu-do also represents one of history's first successful unions of Eastern and Western educational approaches. From the East we find an emphasis on intuitive learning via direct experience and endless repetition of fundamental exercises. We can see the influence of Western practices in Nakamura Sensei's use of detailed lectures and well-thought-out explanations and theories, along with his application of scientific experimentation and concepts.

These are only a few ways that Shin-shin-toitsu-do synthesizes (and transcends) Asian and Western techniques of mind/body coordination, with yoga concepts and practices forming the central backbone of this multi-limbed creation. This explanation is, however, only offered as a means of contrasting Japanese and Indian yoga. It is not motivated out of any sense of competition with traditional yoga, a practice that Nakamura Sensei certainly respected, as do I.

IF YOU ALREADY PRACTICE INDIAN YOGA

When Nakamura Tempu Sensei returned to Japan in 1919 after living in India, he was regarded in some circles as the "father of yoga in Japan." Nevertheless, over time, Shin-shin-toitsu-do became less related to Indian yoga and more its own unique Way. Due to his yogic training in India, Nakamura Sensei certainly had the right to draw parallels between his teachings and Indian traditions, but I must note that contemporary Shin-shin-toitsu-do has definitely evolved into a distinctly *Japanese* form of yoga. Practitioners of Indian yoga shouldn't be surprised if some methods and definitions used in this book do not correspond to what they've previously experienced. This needn't be a problem if we realize that real learning or growth only takes places by encountering the unknown.

We live at a time, in the United States at least, when the term "yoga" has changed into a rather generic title for disciplines that aim at a state of personal integration. It's not uncommon to see books about, for example, "Chinese Taoist yoga." Shin-shin-toitsu-do enthusiasts will therefore sometimes use "Japanese yoga" to broadly describe their study because of Nakamura Sensei's training and because the Sanskrit term "yoga" implies an art for achieving oneness and unification—the goal of Shin-shin-toitsu-do. No attempt is being made here to misappropriate an important Indian cultural property, and in fact, the designation "Japanese yoga" allows us to acknowledge Nakamura Sensei's great debt to the ancient spiritual traditions of India. My associates and I have the same ultimate goal as people who practice classical Indian yoga—to be one with the universe. And at the dawn of a new millennium, when traditional Indian Hatha yoga has sadly sometimes grown so Westernized and watered-down in the United States as to be little more than an esoteric equivalent to aerobics, this is a most important heritage to share.

While I do occasionally draw parallels between Shin-shin-toitsu-do and Indian forms of yoga, I've made no attempt to rigorously back up my general statements about Indian teachings, cite sources, or offer detailed information about the history and theory of these Indian traditional methods. This is simply beyond the scope of this work, which is specifically devoted to a Japanese derivative of yogic techniques.

◆ ◆ ◆

I hope that you will enjoy this book, the first of its kind in English on Nakamura Tempu Sensei and his system of Japanese yoga. More volumes are in the works, and all cover concepts that transcend the given art being discussed—principles that relate to every aspect of living and are genuinely universal.

H. E. Davey
Green Valley, California

ACKNOWLEDGMENTS

An author working in isolation can rarely produce a book.
Several of the students and assistant instructors at the Sennin Foundation Center for Japanese Cultural Arts graciously posed for the illustrations in this book. I'd like to thank Ariel Agress, Alexander Agress, Terri Brown, Ann Kameoka Sensei, Kevin Heard Sensei, and Ohsaki Jun Sensei for their help with this project and for their friendship. In particular, I'm grateful to Steve Aibel for his great photography and well-executed portrait of Nakamura Sensei.

Naturally, I couldn't have written this text without having had excellent Shin-shin-toitsu-do training under equally superb teachers. I've been exceedingly fortunate to practice in the United States and in Japan with various Shin-shin-toitsu-do instructors, including four of Nakamura Tempu Sensei's top students: the late Hirata Yoshihiko Sensei, the late Tohei Koichi Sensei, Sawai Atsuhiro Sensei, and Hashimoto Tetsuichi Sensei. Hashimoto Sensei and Sawai Sensei serve as Senior Advisors to the Sennin Foundation Center. My association with these men permanently changed my life.

My late father, Victor H. Davey, and my late mother, Elaine, supported me both in my life and in my study of Japanese yoga. A debt such as this can never be repaid, but it can be acknowledged.

It's due to my involvement in Shin-shin-toitsu-do that I met Ann Kameoka, my wife and coauthor of our book, *The Japanese Way of the*

Flower: Ikebana as Moving Meditation. From the time Ann came as a student to my dojo (training hall) in the early 1980s, she has been a constant source of help . . . in every aspect of my life.

A NOTE ON THE JAPANESE LANGUAGE

Japanese is the international language of the Japanese cultural arts and meditative Ways. In many cases, a single word in Japanese can have many different shades of meaning. For example, the Japanese word *kokoro* can alternately mean "mind," "spirit," "soul," "heart," or "energy," and even imply "emotion" or "feeling." Therefore, it is often preferable to use native Japanese terms rather attempt a single English equivalent.

Shin-shin-toitsu-do, or Japanese yoga, is not merely a health exercise or form of meditation. It is a Japanese cultural art. A moderate knowledge of the Japanese language, acquired during your yoga practice, can thus open certain doors, leading to a deeper understanding of Japan and making the study of its cultural activities more meaningful.

Some familiarity with the Japanese language also allows the Western enthusiast to more easily interact with Japanese experts (and bona fide Western authorities) without fear of embarrassment. My own modest knowledge of Japanese customs and terminology has even proved to be a mutual connection between myself and non-English-speaking individuals from other Western countries. We were able to share a common bond—the language of the Japanese cultural arts.

To properly pronounce the Japanese words in this book, follow the the guidelines below.

a is pronounced "ah" as in *father*

e is pronounced "eh" as in *Edward*

i is pronounced "ee" as in *police*

o is pronounced "oh" as in *oats*

u is pronounced "oo" as in *tune*

Double consonants are spoken with a brief break between syllables. In Japanese, *r* is pronounced as a mix of the English *r* and *l*. The special orthographic signs called macrons, used in some books to indicate extended vowel sounds in Japanese, are not used here.

When talking or writing in Japanese, it is customary to place the family (last) name first and the given (first) name second. This convention has, with one or two exceptions, been observed in this book. In some cases, the Japanese pronunciations of Chinese words and proper names are used, as are "non-standard" romanized spellings of common or well-established Japanese names. *Sensei*, a Japanese appellation of respect that means "teacher," is invariably placed after a professor's family name. It is used in an identical manner to the honorific suffix -*san*.

UCHU-REI: "universal mind," painted in the style of Kobara Ranseki Sensei. Nakamura Sensei realized that human beings are "lords of creation" in that only mankind is aware of being born and that we will die. While plants and animals are one with the universe, equal to men and women, only humans seem to have the capacity to act upon this realization. Within humanity are reflexive characteristics common to plants and emotional characteristics that can be witnessed in the animal world. But unlike plants and animals, humankind has a capacity for reason rarely duplicated in animals. This "thinking ability" can lead humanity away from its original, naturalistic state. But it also allows us to consciously realize our innate unity with the universe, an ability that Nakamura Sensei called uchu-rei, the "universal mind."

Chapter 1

NAKAMURA TEMPU & THE ORIGINS OF JAPANESE YOGA

Indian forms of yoga have spread throughout the world due to their objectives of promoting health and harmony. Japan is but one of many countries that have received these age-old teachings. While Indian yogic disciplines (Hatha yoga in particular) have become well known, not everyone realizes that certain distinctive Japanese versions of Indian spiritual paths have evolved. Perhaps the first of these unique methodologies is the art of Shin-shin-toitsu-do, which was developed by Nakamura Tempu Sensei (1876–1968). In fact, Nakamura Sensei is often considered to be the father of yoga in Japan.

Nakamura Tempu Sensei was born Nakamura Saburo in Oji in northern Tokyo, a member of the aristocratic Tachibana family, part of the Yanagawa clan of Kyushu. The young Nakamura's mother and father enrolled him, starting at the age of six, in judo and *kendo* (a sword-based martial sport) classes. He excelled in both. He also studied

Zuihen Ryu *batto-jutsu*, a classical system of swordsmanship, for many years. Always interested in things of a spiritual nature, young Nakamura practiced a variety of native Japanese Ways (Do), and he investigated traditional Japanese healing arts. He would remain interested in both of these throughout his life.

After completing his primary education he traveled to his father's place of birth in Fukuoka. There he attended a fairly prestigious school renowned for its instruction in English, a language skill that would prove useful on his journeys later in life. But despite his active participation in various Do forms, young Nakamura had a violent temper that worried his family. Hoping to curb his behavior, his parents encouraged his involvement in the Genyosha, a political organization. As a result of this association, just before the Sino-Japanese War broke out in 1894, Nakamura went to China to engage in Japanese reconnaissance. He went on another reconnaissance sortie to Manchuria just before the onset of the Russo-Japanese War of 1904. Due to his prior training in Japanese swordsmanship, the agent Nakamura earned quite a reputation for fearlessness in battle.

Real understanding is not the mere accumulation of knowledge. Understanding cannot be realized by listening or reading about the realization of others. It must be achieved firsthand via substantive direct perception in the moment.

On a subsequent trip to China, he contracted tuberculosis, which in those days was frequently a fatal disease; the army doctor who made this diagnosis gave him only six months to live. Despite Nakamura Sensei's knowledge of certain traditional Japanese healing methods, his condition worsened. He went to the United States in the early 1900s

24

to receive Western-style medical treatment, and initially it seemed to cure him. Impressed with the effectiveness of the treatments he received, Nakamura Sensei enrolled in Columbia University, where he studied medicine.

A Search Begins

Nakamura Sensei, however, began to cough up blood again. Despite his past training in various Japanese spiritual paths, he had over the years become almost totally preoccupied with the body—his body in particular. Realizing this, and perhaps feeling that he had gone as far as he could with different "body-oriented cures," he decided to explore the mind as a possible means of curing his illness. Inspired by Thomas Edison's claim that his famed discoveries weren't due to academic training but were the outcome of carefully observing the true nature of everyday events, Nakamura Sensei felt that his cure might lie within his own mind, and that it might be discovered in daily existence.

He renewed his study of different Japanese spiritual paths. Yet after his medical training in America, he felt that truth was not limited to Japan. He began to read a variety of what are known today as "self-help books," including *How to Get What You Want* by Orison Swett Marden. There was no real change in him.

He tried a health improvement system called Motion Motive with little result. He heard of a philosopher who had successfully treated an illness that had befallen Edison using psychosomatic medicine. Through this philosophy, Nakamura Sensei formulated a theory of spiritual transformation and non-materialism that would stay with him for the rest of his life . . . but he was still plagued by a life-threatening illness.

Nakamura Tempu Sensei even traveled to England to study with H. Addington Bruce, who had evolved his own form of personal growth. Bruce encouraged him to transcend worry and forget useless things. It was, again, something that he would later transmit to his own students . . . but he was still coughing.

Since he was already in Europe, he decided to explore the depths of the newly developing field of psychology, and he would later use the general concepts he had learned in his teaching of Japanese yoga. His study of psychology spanned France, Germany, and Belgium . . . but he still couldn't shake the tuberculosis.

Despite believing even more strongly in the possibility of a psychosomatic cure, Nakamura Sensei met with no success. Despondent, he decided to return to Japan. But he would stop in Egypt first.

A Turning Point

In Cairo, while staying in a local hotel, an Indian yogi named Kaliapa (also, Kariappa) befriended him. Upon the urging of his new mentor, Nakamura Sensei decided to make a quick detour—a detour that resulted in his traveling to the Himalayas around 1916. It would be about three years, and a new life later, before he returned to Japan.

Nakamura Sensei and Kaliapa ended up on Mt. Kanchenjunga, at 28,146 feet the third highest mountain in the world. Kaliapa taught various yogic methods, but more than this, he created an environment in which Nakamura Sensei ceased to look for answers in books, theories, or the belief systems of others. Kaliapa, using psychological techniques that Nakamura Sensei recalled as being severe, encouraged his student to search for firsthand understanding that was not dependent on any authority or system.

To summarize Kaliapa's position is fairly simple: we are one with the universe, we are therefore imbued with the energy of the universe (*ki* in Japan, *prana* in India), and, as a result, we can learn directly from the universe itself.

Kaliapa told Nakamura Sensei that he depended too much on the teachings of others, and his illness was actually a blessing in disguise since it forced him to consider the real nature of his existence. Nevertheless, if he was to go any further in life, it was time to forget about living and dying. Kaliapa observed that since it was impossible to know exactly when one would die, Nakamura Sensei should stop worrying about death and live each day fully.

What's more, Kaliapa noted that the body reflects the mind and emotions. In a way, the mind is comparable to the source of a river, and the body is like the downstream currents. Consequently, Kaliapa stressed that even if the body falls ill, the mind must remain positive and vigorous or our physical condition will be further debilitated by our attitude. He even suggested that the specific condition of certain internal organs was an indication of related emotional problems.

Kaliapa frequently offered up questions but provided no answers to be memorized. Among these inquiries was a single question that Nakamura Tempu Sensei would reflect on incessantly, and which had a tremendous transformative effect on him: "What are men and women born into this life to do?"

Nakamura Sensei's realization led him to state that human beings are "lords of creation" because only humans are aware of their births

NAKAMURA TEMPU AND THE ORIGINS OF JAPANESE YOGA

and their mortality. Even more important, while plants and animals are undoubtedly one with the universe, equal to men and women, only humans have the capacity to consciously realize this fact and act upon it. Within humanity are reflexive characteristics common to plants and emotional characteristics witnessed in animals, but unlike plants and animals, humans have a highly evolved capacity for reason that is rarely duplicated in the animal world. This "thinking ability" can lead humanity away from its original, naturalistic state, but it also gives us the capacity to consciously and directly realize our innate unity with the universe, an ability that Nakamura Tempu Sensei called *uchu-rei*, the "universal mind." In 1919, Nakamura Sensei returned to Japan . . . and he never coughed up blood again.

A New Beginning and a New Teaching

Nakamura Sensei entered the business world of Tokyo with his characteristic zeal. In time, he would become the Chief Director of the Tokyo Jitsugyo Chozo Bank and serve on the Board of Directors of the Dai Nihon Seifun Milling Company. He taught a synthesis of the various arts, skills, and meditations he had learned, but only on a private basis. Gradually, however, he began to teach more and more publicly. Each morning, he would offer free instruction in Hibiya and Ueno parks. His first organization was called the Toitsu Tetsuigakkai. Eventually, the Tempu-Kai, or "Tempu Society," grew up around him, and it was formally inaugurated in 1962.

Since he stressed the unification of mind and body, he termed his teachings "Shin-shin-toitsu-do," literally, "the Way of mind and body unification." Practioners of this form of Japanese yoga sometimes refer to it is as just Shin-shin-toitsu ("mind and body unification"), as Shin-shin-toitsu-ho ("the art/method of mind and body unification"), or as Toitsu-do ("the Way of unification").* Despite building a following and an organization, Nakamura Sensei was adamant that Shin-shin-toitsu-do be an examination of the very essence of spirituality as opposed to an organized religion of any kind.

What was it that Nakamura Tempu Sensei taught? Based on the fact that the mind and body are one, his comments to others were usually not only of a spiritual nature, but also rather down-to-earth. Here are a few of the topics that he frequently discussed:

- While we can learn or study techniques for almost anything we might want to accomplish, real understanding is not the mere accumulation of knowledge. Understanding cannot be realized by listening or reading about the realization of others. It must be achieved firsthand via substantive, direct perception in the moment.

- By means of personal experimentation and observation, we can discover certain simple and universal truths. The mind moves the body, and the body follows the mind. Logically then, negative thought patterns harm not only the mind but also the body. What we actually *do* builds up to affect the subconscious mind and in turn affects the conscious mind and all reactions.

---

* The real essence of the teaching cannot be contained in a name. In recent years, perhaps the designation Toitsu-do is used less frequently, to avoid being mistaken for Toitsu Kyokai—the Japanese transliteration for the Unification Church. Tempu-kai is a nonprofit educational corporation. It is not a church or temple.

- The young should not think of themselves as immature and the elderly need not view themselves as feeble. Our minds control our bodies. Have no age, transcend both past and future, and enter into *naka-ima*—the "eternal present."

- If we fail to realize our full potential as human beings, we live more on an animalistic level. This is fine for dogs, cats, and chimpanzees but doesn't work quite so well for women and men. Without the capacity to freely shape our own lives, much as a sculptor might carve stone, we inevitably slip into negativity and depression.

- Using the combined, integrated force of the mind and body is more efficient than using one without the other. Since the body can only exist in the present, that's where the mind should be too (unless we deliberately choose to contemplate the past or future). At the same time, the body needs to be healthy and in optimum operating condition so that it can respond effectively to the mind's directives.

- Mental and physical health is more important than money or possessions. Nakamura Sensei had material wealth and was still unable to cure his tuberculosis. Human life power is more meaningful than either cash or houses.

- A strong life force can be seen in physical vitality, courage, competent judgment, self-mastery, sexual vigor, and the realization of each person's unique talents and purpose in life. To maintain a powerful life force, forget yourself, forget about living and dying, and bring your full attention into this moment.

Nakamura Sensei did teach certain techniques of mind and body unification, meditation, breathing exercise, and health improvement that served as simple tools for living a fuller life but should not be thought of as magic secrets of enlightenment. Considering the experiences of his life, we can trace the various influences of Nakamura Sensei's methods.

Historical Influences

Naturally, influences from Indian forms of Hatha, Raja, and Pranayama yoga can be detected, albeit in a usually modified structure. Both *anjo daza ho* and *muga ichi-nen ho* meditations, which we'll explore later, have been influenced by yogic meditation. And while Nakamura Sensei developed his own forms of stretching and physical training, he would periodically teach certain asana (postures) from Hatha yoga, and some types of Pranayama breathing exercises such as the "alternate nostril breath." (I've made a decision in writing this book not to include these practices as they've previously been covered in a variety of works on Hatha yoga and Pranayama.)

Nakamura Sensei's emphasis on experimentation and understanding via direct perception echoes his training in Western science and medicine. He frequently conducted actual scientific experiments to study the effects of Shin-shin-toitsu-do, and to this day leading Western-style physicians in Japan are prominent practitioners of Japanese yoga. *Jiko anji*, his method of autosuggestion (which you'll also have a chance to read about later), is derived from his experiences in the Himalayas, but the explanation is directly borrowed from his study of Western psychology in Europe.

Certainly, various native Japanese influences can be felt in Shin-shin-toitsu-do. Shinto, the indigenous Japanese religion, emphasizes purity and unification with nature, and its influence has permeated every aspect of Japanese culture. Likewise, Zen Buddhism has had a dramatic impact on Japan since its arrival from China around a thousand years ago. Since Nakamura Tempu Sensei grew up and lived within a cultural matrix imbued for centuries with Zen and Shinto, it should come as no surprise that some of the elements and aesthetics of these religions can be encountered in Japanese yoga.

What's more, certain "Japanized" Chinese influences can be found as well. Chinese Taoism has always stressed living in harmony with nature and oneness with the universe. Over time it evolved various meditations and health exercises that aimed at not only enlightenment, but also longevity (and in some cases, outright immortality). Centuries ago, like many aspects of Chinese culture, these teachings migrated to Japan, where Taoism became known as Dokyo.

Taoist mystics, who had attained a high degree of spiritual development and physical vitality, were called *hsien* in China. In Japan, this Chinese character was pronounced *sen* (practitioners were called *sennin*). Esoteric Taoist meditative practices and health-maintenance techniques sometimes come under the general heading of Sennin-do, while arcane Taoist-derived healing arts can be generically termed Sennin Ryoji. The influences of these Taoist methods, which are sometimes dubbed Senjutsu or Sendo, extend to Shin-shin-toitsu-do. More than one author has written that the Taoist sennin, with their meditative practices and health-maintenance techniques, were the Japanese equivalents to the Indian yogi, and their effect is particularly felt in some Shin-shin-toitsu-do breathing exercises and self-healing arts. In particular, the emphasis on the development of life energy in Shin-shin-toitsu-do is paralleled in Chinese Taoist *chi-kung* (*kiko* in Japanese). Shin-shin-toitsu-do in fact can also be thought of as a form of Sennin-do.

> *It's useless to merely copy the original arts that [Nakamura Sensei] studied or to amass a collection of such arts ourselves. Rather, we should directly discover the truth for ourselves as he did.*

While Japanese yoga is certainly not a form of martial arts, Japanese budo nevertheless has had a strong effect on Shin-shin-toitsu-do. Nakamura Sensei was an advanced practitioner of Zuihen Ryu batto-jutsu, a form of Japanese swordsmanship, and the influence of the martial arts can be felt in certain moving exercises, or forms of dynamic meditation, taught in Japanese yoga. He was also from a samurai family and a descendant of Lord Tachibana, a daimyo (feudal lord) in Yanagawa, an area where the martial arts were extremely popular in ancient times.

During the Russo-Japanese War, he used his sword in battle and earned the rather dubious nickname "Man-Cutting Tempu." Yet after returning from India, he stressed love and protection for all creations, and during World War II saved the life of a downed American pilot whom Japanese villagers were beating. While Nakamura Sensei continued to practice solo sword forms for the rest of his life, he was quick to emphasize that he envisioned no enemy while performing batto-jutsu as moving meditation.

His skill with the sword was so great that he frequently demonstrated how he could cleanly cut through a thick piece of bamboo armed with only a wooden sword. Impressive yes, but more impressive still was the fact that the bamboo would be hung from holes cut in two strips of rice paper suspended by two upturned knives held by a couple of assistants. The bamboo would be broken without tearing the suspending top and bottom holes in these strips. (The bamboo was cut in half with such speed that the outer ends would slip from the holes without damaging the paper.) Even more impressive and significant was the fact that Nakamura Sensei was able to teach the average person—including people who had no training in swordsmanship—to do the same thing. He explained that the secret didn't lie in sword technique but rather in coordination of mind and body.

As a side note, when I first met Hashimoto Tetsuichi Sensei, one of Nakamura Sensei's senior students, he demonstrated a similar feat at the *ryokan* (Japanese inn) where my wife and I were staying. Hashimoto Sensei asked me to hold a pair of chopsticks in both hands. He then produced a postcard and, in one sudden swipe, cut cleanly through the chopsticks. The postcard was not damaged. According to Hashimoto Sensei, the secret is either to visualize ki passing through the chopsticks or to believe simply that they had already been broken. After that, it's a matter of relaxing completely and cutting downward without hesitation. This, he taught, would result in a unification of mind and body that was extremely powerful. After a couple of false starts, my wife was able to break the chopsticks as well.

Moving from and focusing power in the *hara*, a natural abdominal center, has a long tradition in both Zen meditation and budo. In some of Nakamura Sensei's moving meditation exercises we can see traces of judo movements as well. And since Nakamura Sensei was a friend of the founder of aikido and had a number of prominent aikido teachers as students, it isn't surprising to see aikido influences in Shin-shin-toitsu-do, particularly in the art's more recent offshoots.*

The mere synthesis of the various arts mentioned above does not, however, result in Shin-shin-toit-su-do, which has as its true goal the direct, immediate perception of existence. We could practice all of the different things that Nakamura Sensei did and yet still not arrive at realization or even come up with the same exercises. Nakamura Sensei had already studied a plethora of unrelated disciplines before going to India. They did him little good. In fact, it was only when he stopped looking for a new "magical cure or teaching" to add to his arsenal of holistic health methods and spiritual arts that he was able to see the bona fide Way of the universe for himself. More than anything, Kaliapa served as a catalyst for this transformation.

Without the capacity to freely shape our own lives, much as a sculptor might carve stone, we inevitably slip into negativity and depression.

Nakamura Sensei's Continuing Influence

It is this direct perception of reality that made Nakamura Sensei helpful to others. To express this perception, he used various exercises

---

*More than one version of Shin-shin-toitsu-do now exists. Nakamura Tempu Sensei's direct students, not all of whom use the label "Shin-shin-toitsu-do" to describe their teachings, formed most of these offshoots. The Ki no Renma of Tada Hiroshi Sensei is but one example.

and arts with which he was familiar, but this is almost incidental. Every person he moved with his words was swayed more by the power of his direct connection with reality than by anything else. It's useless to merely copy the original arts that he studied or to amass a collection of such arts ourselves. Rather, we should directly discover the truth for ourselves as he did.*

Affectionately and informally known to his associates as Tempu Sensei, Nakamura Sensei's unique insight drew a number of famous people to Shin-shin-toitsu-do classes, although not all were well known at the time. Among his students were former Emperor Hirohito, Matsushita Konosuke (Chairman of Matsushita), Kurata Shuzei (President of Hitachi Manufacturing), Sano Jin (President of Kawasaki Industries), Hara Kei (former Prime Minister of Japan), and even John D. Rockefeller III, whom Nakamura Sensei probably met at the bank he ran.

Many years ago, Nakamura Sensei adopted the name Tempu, meaning "the Wind of Heaven." He derived this name from the Sino-Japanese characters *ten* and *fu* (*pu*) that are alternate pronunciations of the characters for *amatsukaze*. The amatsukaze is a formal technique (*kata*) in Zuihen Ryu swordsmanship, at which Tempu Sensei was particularly expert. This appellation also seemed to appeal to his sense of spiritual purpose.

Nakamura Tempu Sensei passed away on December 1, 1968. He

---

* As a side note, a few years ago, a Japanese delegation of Tempu-kai members traveled to the Himalayas to research the Indian roots of their practices. They traced Nakamura Sensei's journey, and after some difficulty they found the area in which he lived. They even found a statue of Kaliapa and practiced Japanese yoga in the same locations that their teacher had so many years before. While all of this made for interesting reading in *Shirube*, the Tempu-kai magazine, no member of the delegation appears to have experienced the same realization as Nakamura Sensei. True understanding cannot be copied.

is buried in Otowa, Tokyo, not too far from where he grew up. For the vast number of people who have knowingly and unknowingly been influenced by his teachings, the Wind of Heaven is still felt rustling through their lives.

NO: *"talent and ability."* Nakamura Tempu Sensei listed no-ryoku, *the capacity for wideranging ability, as an essential aspect of life, indicating that it could be found via unification of mind and body.*

Chapter 2

INTRODUCTION TO MIND & BODY UNIFICATION

FOUR BASIC PRINCIPLES TO UNIFY MIND AND BODY

1. Use the mind in a positive way.

2. Use the mind with full concentration.

3. Use the body naturally.

4. Train the body gradually, systematically, and continuously.

As human beings we seek freedom—political freedom, religious freedom, freedom from discrimination The free use of our minds and bodies—freedom of action in general—is an innate urge.

Each action we take is an act of self-expression. We often think of large-scale or important deeds as being indications of our real selves, but even how we sharpen a pencil can reveal something about our feelings at that moment. Do we sharpen the pencil carefully or nervously so that it doesn't break? Do we bother to pay attention to what we're doing? How do we sharpen the same pencil when we're angry or in a hurry? Is it the same as when we're calm or unhurried?

Even the smallest movement discloses something about the person executing the action because it is the *person* who's actually performing the deed. In other words, action doesn't happen by itself, we make it happen, and in doing so we leave traces of ourselves on the activity. The mind and body are interrelated.

How do you feel when you're unable to express yourself? Imagine you couldn't speak or in some other way communicate. An extreme example perhaps, but how would it feel? In the same way that we suffer if we're unable to express ourselves, we also languish when we cannot, for whatever reason, assert ourselves skillfully. Self-expression is natural, even inevitable, for all of us; and skilled, efficient self-expression goes beyond mere activity and enters the realm of art.

For instance, many of us realize that our handwriting tends to reflect our personalities or at least our state of mind at the moment we put pen to paper. However, when we become conscious of our handwriting as an act of self-expression, when we allow our creativity to flow through the brush or pen in a way that's not only efficient but also coordinated and dexterous, we call what we're doing calligraphy—the art of writing.

Just as writing can become calligraphy when it's creatively, skillfully, and consciously performed, so can all other activities become art. In this case, we are reflecting upon life itself as an artistic statement—the art of living.

From the Particular to the Universal

In Japan, a number of time-honored everyday activities (such as making tea, arranging flowers, and writing) have traditionally been deeply examined by their proponents. Students study how to make tea, perform martial arts, or write with a brush in the most skillful way possible to express themselves with maximum efficiency and minimum strain. Through this efficient, adroit, and creative performance, they arrive at art. But if they continue to delve even more deeply into their art, they discover principles that are truly universal, principles relating to life itself. Then, the art of brush writing becomes shodo—the "Way of the brush"—while the art of arranging flowers is elevated to the status of kado—the "Way of flowers." Through these Ways or Do forms, the Japanese have sought to realize the Way of living itself. They have approached the universal through the particular.

Since the universe is infinite, grasping the ultimate nature of life and the principles of the universe is seemingly a large-scale undertaking. For this reason, it isn't difficult to understand the traditional emphasis on approaching the universal via a profound, ongoing examination of a particular Way. Still, we must wonder if it isn't possible to discover *directly* the essence of living and the universal principles relating to all aspects of life?

Nakamura Tempu Sensei, upon returning from India, shared with others the principles and exercises that he felt were universal and not dependent on a particular art; that is, concepts relating to all activities and all people regardless of age, sex, or race. Methods that have observable and repeatable results, along with principles and exercises that can withstand objective scrutiny, were of primary importance to him.

These concepts and techniques were created to encourage humanity to see into its true nature . . . to realize that life is art. Just as artists can shape clay or brushed images into their vision of beauty, we can shape our lives. But just as artists must acquire certain methods and abilities to effectively create a piece of sculpture or a painting, we need to develop certain qualities of mind and body.

Unification of Mind and Body

No art takes places without inspiration. Every artist also needs effective knowledge of his or her tools (e.g., does a certain brush function well with a particular kind of paint?). What's more, artists need effective techniques for using those tools.

Likewise, to express ourselves skillfully with maximum efficiency and minimum effort, we need to investigate the most effective ways of using the mind and body since, in the end, they are the only "tools" we truly possess in life.

Nakamura Sensei wrote that upon examining life, it's clear that people need six qualities to adeptly express themselves in living:

> *tai-ryoku:* "the power of the body," physical strength, health, and endurance
> *tan-ryoku:* "the power of courage"
> *handan-ryoku:* "the power of decision," good judgment
> *danko-ryoku:* "the power of determination," willpower for resolute and decisive action
> *sei-ryoku:* "the power of vitality," energy or life power for endurance and perseverance

no-ryoku: "the power of ability," the capacity for wideranging ability and dexterous action

More importantly, he realized that since the mind and body represent our most fundamental tools we must be able to use these tools naturally, effectively, and in coordination with each other to artistically express ourselves in life. The ability to effectively use and unite our minds and bodies, our primary components, allows for freedom of action and skilled self-expression.

In the instance of the lungs and various internal organs, the mind exerts unconscious control of the body through the autonomic nervous system. In this system, the mind and body remain unified, and this unity is essential to learning any activity effectively, including Japanese yoga. However, because of this relationship between mind and body, the mind can positively or negatively influence the built-in mind-body connection. (When this tie is weak, you may observe a Japanese yoga exercise demonstrated by a teacher or in a book, fully comprehend it intellectually, and still fail to physically respond in the proper manner.)

Realizing the mind-body relationship, Nakamura Sensei envisioned his basic principles as a means for people to discover for themselves how to coordinate their two most basic tools in life and to learn how to "regulate and strengthen their autonomic nervous systems." Using his background in Western medicine, Nakamura Tempu Sensei conducted biological research dealing with the nervous system and mind and body unification to accomplish this goal. The result was his Four Basic Principles to Unify Mind and Body.

These four principles, which are listed at the beginning of this chapter, are the broad means by which Nakamura Sensei aimed to aid people in uncovering for themselves their true potential and freedom of expression in life. They are a way of discovering that life can be lived as art. Nakamura Sensei also realized that exercises based on these four principles could give people the opportunity to cultivate the above-mentioned six qualities and other important character traits.

The Mind-Body Relationship

I will discuss these four principles and their subprinciples in greater depth in the coming chapters, but for now let me emphasize that the mind controls the body, while the body acts as a reflection of the mind. Let's look at these two statements and attempt to discover if they're true.

What allowed you to read the last few sentences? Did you read them with your eyes? Many of us, without thinking deeply about this question, would respond that we do indeed read a book with our eyes. And while this is certainly true, can we accurately state that it's the whole truth?

Clearly the eyes do not read by themselves. In other words, the body doesn't read. Isn't it the mind that reads through the eyes? In the same vein, the hand does not turn the pages of this book. Does your hand think or direct itself? Perhaps that may occur in horror movies, but in real life the mind turns the page via the hand.

We sometimes say, "Oh, I didn't mean that! I spoke without thinking." Can we really speak without thinking? Does the mouth have free will? Probably not.

Since it is truly the mind that speaks through the mouth, verbal expressions always reveal some aspect of us. Perhaps it's a part of our selves that's buried deeply in the subconscious, but it is nevertheless part of the mind that's being expressed through the body. Think about this seriously, while observing yourself and others to find out if it's actually the case.

If the mind moves and controls the body, then there should be a flip side to this statement. Therefore, if the mind does move the body, we can also say that the body follows the mind.

Suppose you see someone's hand shaking. Further suppose that this person appears to be young and healthy. What would you surmise? We would probably think that the person we're observing is nervous. We arrive at this observation because it's obvious that the body, in this case the hand, acts as a reflection of the mind. And while we may realize this fact, what do we actually do with this knowledge?

Realizing that our minds control our bodies while our bodies reflect our minds amounts to understanding the most fundamental aspects of ourselves. It further equals a comprehension of the relationship between our "tools." And since the mind and body are interrelated, this understanding makes it easier to see why coordinating them is a practical way of using these tools to greatest effect—a way of using the mind and body to live our lives as art.

Moreover, because all actions and expressions stem from the mind, it is vital to know the mind as well as decide in what way we'll use it. Everyone has heard of psychosomatic illness, and most of us acknowledge that psychosomatic sicknesses can and do occur. But what about psychosomatic wellness? How many of us have considered if it's possible to stay healthy or cure various maladies with the positive use of the mind? And if we have thought of this, have we done much more than simply consider the idea? *Japanese Yoga* will give you various

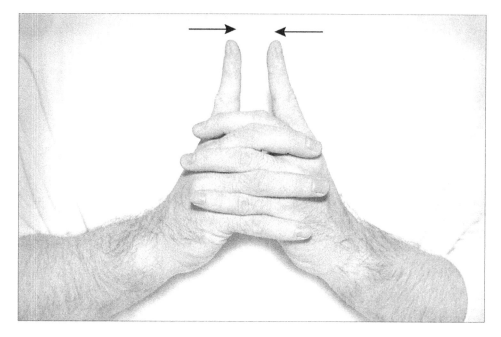

Fig. 1. Experiment One. Interlace your fingers and focus your eyes gently on your fingertips. Move your index fingers together by concentrating.

ideas, principles, and exercises based on the truth that the mind controls the body that can be directly experimented with in daily life. In fact, let's try two experiments dealing with the relationship between the mind and body.

Experimenting with the Mind-Body Connection

EXPERIMENT ONE

Interlace your fingers with the two index fingers extended and apart, as in Figure 1. Keeping your body erect but relaxed, focus your eyes gently on your fingertips. You will attempt to move your index fingers together with the force of your concentration.

You can accomplish this in more than one way. First, try creating a mental image of your fingertips coming together. Next, simply imagine that your fingers are already together and continue to hold that notion in your mind. Third, "talk to yourself," mentally commanding the fingers to touch.

Each of these ideas represents fundamentally the same thought process, but some people have more success with one approach than with another. The central point is to examine whether the power of a concentrated mind can influence the body to automatically respond to whatever thought is in the mind. Since we're experimenting to see if such a response is possible, let's not make any assumptions.

You should avoid having any sensation of deliberately bringing the fingertips together. Rather, merely focus your mind intently on one of the above thoughts or images, sustain this state of attention, and see what happens. If concentration doesn't waver and the body remains relaxed, many people find that their fingers start to move without any intentional effort on their part. This effortless feeling is essentially different from the way many of us move our bodies, and it's one of the secrets to arriving at maximum effectiveness with minimal exertion in Japanese yoga exercises.

On the other hand, because we're experimenting with the effect the mind has on the body, if your concentration weakens, or if you believe that you can't achieve any physiological response by means of concentration, then the fingers may fail to move. In the beginning it may also take some time for the fingers to gradually come together. (This tends to improve with practice.)

Some might note that the index fingers have a natural tendency to come together due to the position of the hands. This is certainly the case. The fact that despite this tendency some individuals fail to cause their fingers to join or can only do so by concentrating for an extended period of time only serves to validate the principle that the mind influences the body. This influence, however, isn't always positive. If we think that we cannot cause the fingers to move with concentration, then the body will fulfill that thought.

Let's try a different version of the same experiment. Realizing that the index fingers actually want to come together, hold them apart and imagine you've placed an invisible rod between the fingertips. Keeping this image in your mind, simply wait. Let 5, even 10, minutes elapse. While you effectively sustain this mental picture, do your fingers come together on their own?

Now, what happens to your fingers over the next several seconds or minutes if you imagine that the rod between your index fingers breaks or falls to the floor?

It's impossible to arrive at a true conclusion by guesswork, which is why actual experiments form the basis of science. Nakamura Sensei, with a background in Western science and medicine, often asked his associates to conduct such experiments. According to Hashimoto Tetsuichi Sensei, one of his top students, he first used the above exercise in the 1920s as a way of illustrating the mind's effect on the body. He emphasized that we understand through real experience. Everything else is mere speculation.

EXPERIMENT TWO

We might surmise that if the mind influences the body, then our mental state should also exert an unconscious influence on whatever the body touches. If this is factual, then our mind can sway everything

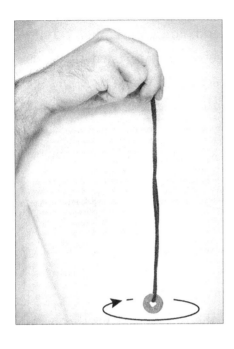

Fig. 2. Experiment Two. Focus your eyes softly on the pendulum. Relax. Imagine the pendulum moving in a clockwise circle, or simply "tell" the pendulum to move. What happens?

from the pool cue we're grasping to the car we're driving. Let's experiment to find out if this is true.

For this experiment, you'll need a pendulum or pendulum-like object. Grip the top of the pendulum string as in Figure 2, and focus your eyes softly on the pendulum. Using the same sort of relaxed concentration described in the first experiment, imagine the pendulum is moving in a clockwise circle. Or simply "tell" the pendulum to move this way. Make every effort to hold your hand still. What happens as you continue to sincerely concentrate?

Frequently, the pendulum will follow your mental dictates whether or not you feel or see your hand moving. Not only does this illustrate the effect the mind has on whatever we come in contact with, but it also shows the extremely subtle effect the mind has on the body. And make no mistake, the mind is moving the pendulum through a remarkably faint motion of the fingers, hand, and arm. Unlike certain occult practices, Nakamura Tempu Sensei never suggested that this was anything other than a humble experiment with which we could see the profound influence the mind has on the body. With practice and increased concentration, it's possible to make the pendulum move in bigger or smaller circles, move sideways, or change direction suddenly—all with little apparent movement of the hand. It's fun to try all of these variations, but don't delude yourself or others into thinking anything supernatural is taking place. It isn't.

Shin-shin-toitsu-do is a study of the principles of nature and how they can be refined to help us realize the truths of nature and our full potentials. While the power and ability released by the practice of Japanese yoga may often exceed the norm ("supernormal"), Nakamura Sensei never aimed at the supernatural. Seeing the genuine heart and principles of the universe is miraculous enough.

Because all actions and expressions stem from the mind, it is vital to know the mind as well as decide in what way we'll use it. Everyone has heard of psychosomatic illness, and most of us acknowledge that psychosomatic sicknesses can and do occur. But what about psychosomatic wellness?

It's also interesting to note the effect of fatigue, depression, happiness, or other conditions on our ability to achieve results in these two experiments. The force of our concentration should be the motivating factor in these exercises. Bearing this in mind, is it possible to discover through direct experience the characteristics of concentration and the positive use of the mind by performing the above experiments repeatedly? Can practicing such tests of the mind-body connection enhance our power of attention? There's only one way to find out.

50

An Objective Approach to Universal Truths

Through direct, unbiased observation and experimentation we can see the various aspects of the universe as they really are. Approaching the principles that govern all sentient life and functions of the universe is fairly simple. A universal truth should be, on some level, detectable. If we cannot see how a principle or concept functions, we really can't validly say anything about it with certainty. At the least, we should be able to observe its functioning through inference. For example, we can't see oxygen, but we can see a candle's flame die when we cover it with a glass. We still can't see the oxygen, but we can see how oxygen, or the lack of it, affects fire. Likewise, we can't see the wind, but we can see the effect of the wind on leaves rustling in the trees.

Experimentation is a way of observing nature. Nevertheless, if we conclude by the above two experiments that the mind moves the body, this would not be a sound conclusion in that it's based on our personal experience alone. Only when other people try the same experiment and arrive at similar results can we begin to form a judgment. Not only should we be able to see tangible results from our own experimentation but also from that of others. In short, that which is true is repeatable.

However, even observable and repeatable results do not automatically qualify something as being universally true. For that, the experiment must be observable and repeatable on a universal scale. When people of all ages in all parts of the world regardless of gender, race, or religion can generally arrive at the same results we can consider a principle or concept to be universal in scope.

Shin-shin-toitsu-do is concerned with principles that are genuinely universal and relate to all aspects of living. Nakamura Sensei's experiments, more of which will be detailed later, are designed to help us personally experience principles that are perceptible, repeatable, and universal. During his lifetime, Nakamura Sensei continued to experiment with the exercises and concepts outlined in this book. While he drew certain "conclusions" from his study, he didn't view these conclusions as an end, and as a result he changed and refined his program of practice on a regular basis throughout his life. In other words, Nakamura Sensei continued to learn.

We can do likewise as long as our minds are not stuck on past conclusions and remain in the present. Then, through the above experiments (for instance), we can see with our own eyes the effect the mind has on the fingers or the pendulum. If we try these exercises several times, we can observe that the results are repeatable. By observing our environment, reading, and watching the results of others, we can discover whether or not they're universal.

In other words, the fact that the mind moves the body while the body follows the mind is something that can be seen and felt, not just once or twice, but over and over by people everywhere. It isn't something that's only valid for certain people in a certain place at a certain time. Other Japanese yoga experiments, some of which will be introduced in subsequent chapters, also confirm this. But don't take my word for it. Try to find out whether this is actually the case by seeing if the other concepts outlined in *Japanese Yoga* are also observable, repeatable, and universal.

Because the mind controls the body, Nakamura Sensei placed the two principles for the mind at the beginning of his Four Basic Principles to Unify Mind and Body. In fact, of the four concepts, number one—"use the mind positively"—should be given greatest priority. In the following chapter, we can consider together the actual characteristics of the conscious and subconscious aspects of the mind. In addition, I'll explain Nakamura Tempu Sensei's Five Principles for a Positive Mind as well as a method of autosuggestion for eliminating negativity.

Seeing the roots of our negativity is vital. Without a positive attitude, we'll rarely have the perseverance or incentive to thoroughly investigate, let alone follow through and comprehend, any practice. If we think that it's too difficult to remember four different principles, that we will never succeed anyway, that we aren't smart enough to figure all of this out, we may fail to even get to principles two, three, and four. In short, without a positive mind, we give up before we start.

SHIN, KOKORO: "mind," painted to resemble a "brain wave." Mind and body are in many ways opposite from each other, and mind and body must each act according to its own principles. Nonetheless, while the mind and body are different in disposition, they are complementary opposites that form a single whole. For us to sustain mind and body harmony, and function as whole human beings, we need to discover the actual nature of the mind's characteristics.

Chapter 3

PRINCIPLES
OF THE MIND

We've all heard of the power of positive thinking, but what is this power and does it actually work? It's impossible to answer this without direct experience and research. To attribute any power to positive thinking is as flawed in reasoning as to assume that no such power exists. Both assumptions are just that—*assumptions*.

Assuming is easy. We simply base our thinking on what we've previously thought, heard, or believed. We can also center our thinking on what we hope to be true but which we haven't actually discovered for ourselves. Likewise, we can believe what everyone else believes, again without any independent verification. All of this is secondhand knowledge. We don't have direct experience and don't personally know if it was true, is true, or ever will be true. We *assume*, instead of uncovering the truth ourselves, as it is at this moment.

In this chapter, let's examine together the genuine meaning of being positive, the possibility of achieving such a state, and the influence it can have on our lives. Let us, moreover, investigate the actual characteristics of concentration. We may have heard that the strength of the mind is related to concentration, but what exactly does this mean? Is concentration the ability to block out all external stimuli and focus on one matter? Or is concentration something else? We can look seriously at these questions right now, and Shin-shin-toitsu-do can help us begin. What's more, let's use the experiences and methods of Naka-mura Sensei not as something to copy but as a catalyst to discover the actual nature of reality.

PRINCIPLE #1: USE THE MIND IN A POSITIVE WAY

To use the mind positively is the first of the Four Basic Principles to Unify Mind and Body (Shin-shin-toitsu no Yondai Gensoku). In many ways, the positive and dynamic use of the mind is the most important point in learning Shin-shin-toitsu-do because without it we may fail to master other aspects of physical and mental training. Con-sider as well the ways in which a negative attitude can influence the body (e.g., psychosomatic sickness).

On the other hand, to be positive in Japanese yoga and life is not to be inflexible or hardheaded, as this contradicts the very nature of *toitsu*, which implies harmony. Actually, a truly positive mind has confi-dence in a positive outcome to most events and is therefore capable of being peaceful, adaptable, and harmonious in response to all circum-stances. In essence, it makes no assumptions about the future, so nega-tivity doesn't arise. As it can confidently handle all situations, a positive mind has no reason to be upset or to resist. This state has been described as *fudoshin* ("immovable mind"), which once again is not inflexibility, but rather a condition of mental stability.

When the mind is positive, the integration of mind and body is maintained, and we're able to manifest our full potential. A negative mind will unconsciously withdraw from action taking place which it does not "feel good about." This creates a separation of mind and body, making us unable to respond effectively in a crisis or when faced with important work. In Shin-shin-toitsu-do, it's vital to throw 100 percent of ourselves into the moment at hand, and this positive mental state is called *ki no dashikata*, or "the projection of life energy."

We've all met exceptionally positive and animated individuals, people who project a "large presence." The intangible but unmistakable "big presence" that an energetic individual projects can be thought of as universal life energy, and it's an indispensable aspect of Shin-shin-toitsu-do.

Releasing Ki

In Japan, the universal essence that pervades nature has a name. It is called "ki."

An understanding of ki cannot be fully detailed in a book, although it will be addressed at length later. For the moment, remember that ki amounts to the animating force that vitalizes all creations, and that positive use of the mind sets it free, while negativity causes *ki ga nukeru*— "the withdrawal and loss of ki."

Ki has been characterized in a variety of ways by an equally wide variety of writers. For the intent of this book, we're thinking of ki as the essential building block of nature, that universal substance from which all things emanate, exist as, and revert to—the connective membrane of the absolute universe. (Of course, just as cells in your body are inseparable from your body, we can only draw an artificial separation between the ki that links all creations in nature and nature itself.)

Unfortunately, discussions of ki are frequently couched in mythi-cal tones, and some writers have suggested that ki is invisible. This depends on your point of view. Certainly it's hard to observe ki as something apart and different from the boundless different aspects of nature. (We probably wouldn't say, for instance, that a truly despicable ki cut us off on the freeway. However, the person who cut in front of us is a manifestation of ki as are other aspects of creation.)

We're commonly looking at the universe based on a relative world-view—a dualistic way of perceiving the cradle of humanity. Of course, relativity and duality exist. If everything is one and that's all there is to it, then why does it hurt when you accidentally hit your finger with a hammer? Clearly, enough of a separation and distinction exist for the hammer to mangle your finger.

A nondualistic worldview does not reject the relative world but sees the absolute oneness of nature that underlies all relative differ-ences. In this case, a willow tree is ki, as is the blustering wind that causes the tree to lean. And we are ki watching the motion of ki in the universe which is ki itself. The wind blowing the willow, the swaying tree, the mind that sees and moves with the wind and willow—all are reflections of diversified elements of ki, the sum total of the universe. (In *Japanese Yoga*, the word "universe" has a much more profound meaning than a collection of stars and planets.) Ki is not preternatural, invisible, or elusive—it is all encompassing.

So, if ki amounts to "everything," why use the word at all? The answer lies in a nondualistic perception of existence. We perhaps have no word in English as all encompassing, far-reaching, and universal as ki. And in the exploration of nondualistic perception, the term ki can be a useful tool, causing us to consider ordinary aspects of life in a different way than we're accustomed to doing. But the word is only a tool. It's not a marketing gimmick, a device with which to impress others, or a catchall buzzword uttered to hide a lack of real understanding. (And it's been used, and sometimes continues to be used, in all of those ways.)

Ki's far-reaching and down-to-earth spirit* is reflected in the Japanese language that employs this ordinary term in a seemingly immeasurable number of compound words and expressions, a few of which are listed below:

> *yuki*: courage, literally "active ki"
> *ki ga shizumu*: depression, "ki sinks down"

---

* Kouzo Kaku Sensei's book *The Mysterious Power of Ki: The Force Within* (Folkestone, Kent: Global Oriental, 2000) features Mr. Nakamura and Shin-shin-toitsu-do prominently, indicating that Nakamura Sensei was one of Japan's earliest and most influential researchers into the nature of ki. In particular, it documents Nakamura Sensei's role in studying the relationship between the mind and ki.

According to Kouzo Sensei, Mr. Nakamura felt that the positive or negative use of the mind had a profound impact not only on our bodies, but also on the action of ki. Nakamura Tempu frequently said that he was echoing traditional yogic philosophy by explaining that "the active thinking of the mind creates one's life."

Kouzo Sensei suggests that when Mr. Nakamura encountered this philosophy in India, he was somewhat baffled as to its ultimate meaning. Over time, as he reflected on his illness and the meaning of human life, he realized the way in which the mind functions in turn influences the way an individual's life force behaves . . . a life force that is continuously received by human beings from the universe. This ki, or "life energy," is received not only by the brain, but flows through the nervous system, thus animating the body and the mind. Nakamura Sensei felt that the absolute ki of the universe is one and without duality, but that when it manifests in the relative world, it takes on relative characteristics. Therefore, ki can display a constitution that is life-giving or destructive, positive or negative, strong or weak, hard or soft. Once negative ki is activated via negative thought patterns, in the course of our lives we will attract further negative ki and circumstances. A positive mind, similarly, activates positive ki that will be projected into a person's daily life and engender good fortune.

Also according to *The Mysterious Power of Ki*, Mr. Nakamura taught that ki existed in the relative world in many forms—such as electricity and magnetic power—but that all of these different varieties of ki were multiform aspects of a single, absolute, original energy sometimes characterized as *seiki, senten no ikki*, or *uchu-rei*. Depending on their religion, others may here use terms like God or Allah.

ki ga kiku: cleverness, "ki works sharply"

ki o tobasu: frightened, "ki flies away"

tenki: weather, "the ki of heaven"

kuki: air, "the ki of emptiness"

Nakamura Tempu Sensei taught at length about ki and its relationship to the union of mind and body. His teachings in many ways echo those of the originators of a number of the Do forms, including shodo (brush calligraphy), kado (flower arrangement), and budo (martial arts).

Nakamura Tempu Sensei viewed the mind as a segment of the body that could not be seen and the body as the element of the mind that was observable. He also likened the mind and body to a stream, with the mind as the source flowing down to the body. Whatever we drop in the stream will be carried down by the current. In like manner, our thoughts will influence the body and our well being.

Orenai Te

Ki can be seen not only as the connective tissue of creation, but also as the uniting component between mind and body. Just as ki is observable in nature through its reflections (i.e., the boundless actions of nature's infinite number of integral parts), so too is the movement of ki visible as a reflection on the body. Nevertheless, this discussion can easily become empty philosophy. Hashimoto Tetsuichi has indicated that Nakamura Sensei invented a matter-of-fact exercise called *orenai te* to allow students to experiment with the relationship between the mind and body, the innate power of mind-body coordination, and the reflected motion of ki. *Orenai* means something that cannot be bent or collapsed, while *te* relates to your hand or arm.

Since most Japanese arts, including Shin-shin-toitsu-do, value the positive cultivation of ki as well as the unity of body and mind, it wasn't unusual to find highly regarded instructors of other disciplines in Naka-mura Tempu Sensei's classes. As a result, the orenai te exercise has found its way into a number of widespread disciplines, especially the martial arts (aikido in particular) and the healing arts. (It has also, in some instances, been taught with mysterious overtones not encoun-tered in Nakamura Sensei's original no-nonsense presentation.)

EXPERIMENT THREE

You'll need a friend to help you investigate orenai te. Stretch out one arm about shoulder height, parallel to the ground. Make a tight fist and stiffen your arm in an attempt to make it unyielding. Your partner grips your wrist with one hand and the bend of your elbow with the other. He or she should try to gradually collapse your arm by pushing your wrist back toward your shoulder while the other hand presses down into the bend of your elbow. Try to keep your arm rigid and cen-ter your mind on where your friend is touching you. Unless your part-ner is quite a bit physically weaker than you are, the muscular strength of two arms will readily defeat the opposition of one arm.

Next, test a different approach. Relax your arm, open your hand, and leave a natural bend in your elbow, but make sure you do not fall completely limp. Then, picture a river of ki running through your arm, out of your extended fingertips, through whatever is in front of you, and continuing endlessly. (Using a mental picture of light being pro-jected may help you.) Rather quickly, you'll no longer be able to men-

Fig. 3. Experiment Three: Orenai Te. Your partner applies pressure using two hands—one holding your inner elbow and one grasping your wrist—and gradually presses your wrist back toward your shoulder. Try various responses: muscular tension and resistance, limpness and resignation, and bodily suppleness and the mental picture of a line of ki that continues indefinitely.

tally track the image of ki as it will reach a point too far away to intellectually visualize. At that time, do nothing, and allow the feeling of ki pouring out to proceed on its own.

Have your friend gradually, so as not to upset your concentration, bend your arm using exactly the same measure of effort as before. Providing your current of attention is undisturbed and your body remains relaxed, the arm should be largely unaffected by your partner's pressure as in Figure 3. Bear in mind that this is a comparative not a competitive exercise. Your partner should use equivalent power both times for an accurate comparison.

You can also explore letting your body droop limply while your partner tries to collapse your arm. I think you'll find this is as unproductive as tensing your body in response to pressure.

Note the following hints:

- Your partner can apply pressure most readily using two hands—one holding the inner elbow and one grasping the wrist and pressing it in its natural direction back toward the shoulder.

- Employ pressure gradually, calmly, and with complete awareness on the part of both participants.

- As your partner applies pressure, try responding to the force in the following three ways:

    1. Use muscular tension and resistance.

    2. Use limpness and resignation.

    3. Use a fusion of a supple body and the mental picture of a line of ki that flows from your fingertips and continues into the universe indefinitely.

The first approach amounts to setting up a barrier of resistance between you and nature. (Keep in mind that your friend is as much a part of nature as you are.) Using the second method is similar to withdrawing psychologically from nature, while the last way involves an act of unification that is unusually powerful. In this condition of unification, you neither fight back nor withdraw. Instead, you let your ki combine with the ki in nature. At the same time, your mind is moving in the identical direction as your fingers are pointing, and as a result, the mind and body are harmoniously joined in the same place at the same time.

Uniting the mind and body is needed for performing the exercises in this book. If your mind accurately sees the illustrations but your body is incapable of demonstrating the coordination to efficiently duplicate them, no immediate success is possible. In other words, a gap between your mind and body will result in a disagreement between your thoughts and your actions. When ki flows without restraint, mind and body are harmonized, and your body will correctly recreate what your mind sees.

Use of ki in orenai te functions on two levels: mental and physical. Both are important, and it's difficult to determine where the mind ends and the body starts since they are interconnected. Tension weakens the body because your muscles are fighting against each other. Limpness is also ineffective because your muscles and body parts are disjointed from each other. Either condition amounts to "the withdrawal of ki" (ki ga nukeru) and a lack of personal harmony.

Similarly, focusing your attention on your partner's hands holding your arm traps the mind and ki at those points. Conversely, guiding your attention in the identical direction that your fingertips are pointing releases ki. Keeping your posture and arm in a supple but not slack condition also helps your body to best respond to your mind. Transferring the psychophysical lessons encountered in orenai te is important for success in the disciplines to come and for using Shin-shin-toitsu-do in everyday life as moving meditation.

You can try another orenai te experiment by extending your arm once more in a relaxed but not flaccid way. First, envision an outward movement of ki that continues endlessly to join with the ki of nature. Your arm will most likely be as unbending as before. While your friend continues to try to push your wrist back to your shoulder, abruptly think of sucking ki back into your arm. At the moment many people think of pulling in ki (withdrawing psychologically from nature), their arm collapses. Their partner just needs to sustain his or her effort.

In this case, your friend's power and your arm's condition are the same. The difference is in the movement of the mind and ki. But this activity of ki is not contingent on a visualized image, and in fact such an image will ultimately be an obstacle. Clearly, we cannot realistically function throughout the day holding onto a specific mental picture. The mind needs to be free to focus upon activity that's taking place in the instant. It is therefore critical that we learn to let the visualization fade as it moves too far away to imagine while still sustaining the flow of ki and the condition of mind-body coordination. As this mental image is dropped, only uncorrupted attention remains.

THE PURPOSE OF ORENAI TE

It's the state of pure attention and unification that's meaningful when experimenting with orenai te. This exercise is not meant to cultivate otherworldly strength, to impress friends, or to advertise the power of ki. Writer Dave Lowry has correctly noted that some serious practitioners of Japanese Do forms have grown irritated with "the over-mystification of ki which has become practically a cottage industry among many authors bent on draping Japan's artistic forms in impenetrable mysticism." And so they should. Our natural universe is miraculous just as it is, and humanity's failure to see this truth is the source of much dissatisfaction in the world. Nakamura Sensei considered comprehension of ki to be only one of numerous important aspects of Japanese yoga.

In spite of what some books have claimed, orenai te is nothing mysterious, it isn't literally "unbendable," and it in no way goes beyond the physical laws of nature. No occult-like energy is involved. A change takes place in the way the muscles function when orenai te is accurately performed that makes the arm exceptionally difficult to bend. The integrated use of the mind and body actually heightens the muscular power of the arm.

While not preternatural, this experiment can explain by example how mind, body, and nature are interconnected and how "reaching out" with ki to unify with nature can cause results that are reflected on material realities (the body, in this instance). Orenai te not only gives us a chance to experience a different manner of dealing with the world—a way that's at once harmonious and powerful—but it also suggests a tangible means of encountering a union of mind, body, and nature. Shin-shin-toitsu-do's ultimate purpose is a condition of oneness, and this exercise can perhaps give yoga aficionados an alternative means to a mental and physical state that lies at the core of their Way.

In addition, orenai te is a method of looking at the meaningful qualities that are customarily valued in the Japanese cultural arts and generally in daily living. To begin with, orenai te uses positive and powerful imagery to encourage a parallel positive physical condition. We've heard of the deep effect the mind can have on the body, but not everyone has directly experimented with this effect. Orenai te offers just such an opportunity.

It also gives us a chance to analyze the power of concentration. Obviously, it's easy to lose concentration or self-assurance if a large individual aggressively tries to collapse your arm—especially if this takes place in front of others. With the loss of concentration, confidence, or belief, your arm crumples. But with sustained study, it's possible to amplify our ability to positively concentrate even during activity or under pressure.

On a physical level, the arm is neither tense nor limp, and the same holds true for our overall physical carriage. A collapsed, diminutive manner or an inordinately erect, tense posture are equally unproductive for carrying out orenai te successfully. They're also debilitating in everyday life, and unfortunately many of us seem to waver eternally between moments of disproportionate tension and exhausted collapse. We're frequently unsure of how to use our bodies naturally in a condition of functional relaxation. Once more, orenai te gives us a chance to experiment with the most natural and effective use of the body (within the context of a given practice). This is indispensable in Shin-shin-toitsu-do, where some exercises can be physically demanding. A Shin-shin-toitsu-do practitioner cannot functionally perform in a condition of mental and physical limpness. On the other hand, sustaining tension is rough on your health and your Japanese yoga exercises. What's required is positive relaxation—a state of being that's natural and comfortable but still functional.

Glance again at the Four Basic Principles to Unify Mind and Body. Notice that the qualities mentioned above in connection with orenai te are none other than Nakamura Sensei's basic principles for mind and body coordination. Orenai te was created to let us experience these principles for ourselves in a way that transcends mere theory.

Just as in science, however, discovering certain new and significant principles isn't enough. If these principles never find their way into ordinary usage to enhance society as a whole, they have little value to the average person. Similarly, experimenting with orenai te is just that—an experiment. If we fail to investigate how to use our bodies naturally, sustain a positive attitude, and focus the mind, we also fail to derive much real world benefit from the above exercise. It becomes nothing more than a party trick that has little relationship to daily living.

Once we see the advantages of positivity, concentration, and a natural, relaxed posture, it's vital to train the mind and body in a well-organized, gradual, and ongoing manner to actualize these attributes. Shin-shin-toitsu-do, along with the classical Japanese Ways, presents us with an occasion to train ourselves in exactly this manner. But it's just an opportunity. It is up to us to do it.

Cultivating the mind and body in a gradual and continuous way, using the mind positively and energetically, bringing the mind's full attention into the instant while using the body naturally—these points connect to orenai te. But more than that, they equal a pragmatic action plan aiming at mind-body harmony in Japanese yoga and life.

Five Principles for a Positive Mind

1. Examine the self

2. Analyze suggestions received from your environment

3. Examine your attitude toward others

4. Discover the present, and let worrying about the future or the past fall away

5. Experience the universal mind

EXAMINE THE SELF

A positive attitude is most easily arrived at through a deliberate and rational analysis of what's required to manifest unwavering positive thought patterns. First, reflect on the actual, present condition of your mind. In other words, is the mind positive or not? We've all met individuals who perceive themselves as positive people but don't appear as such. Since the mind is both invisible and intangible, it's therefore easier to see the accurate characteristics of the mind through a person's words, deeds, and posture.

For example, if we say, "It's absolutely freezing today! I'll probably catch a cold before the end of the day!" then our words expose a negative attitude. But if we say, "The temperature is very cold" (a simple statement of fact), then our expressions, and therefore attitude, are not negative. Sustaining an alert state in which self-awareness becomes possible gives us a chance to discover the origins of negativity. In doing so, we also have an opportunity to arrive at a state of positiveness, so that our words and deeds are also positive, making others feel comfortable, cheerful, and inspired.

Is being positive to always smile and say that everything's great? Or is it something else? While smiling is one of life's great pleasures, the state of positivity doesn't preclude criticism and commenting on destructive behavior. It doesn't mean that we must always say "yes" instead of "no."

To say no to poverty, racism, violence, pollution, and other social ills isn't being negative—it's being intelligent. To speak the truth with the strength of our entire being is an extremely positive and vigorous action . . . even if the truth is less than pleasant.

To project ki fully into whatever we're doing, to act vigorously with the entire force of the mind and body, to throw 100 percent of ourselves into the moment—this is being positive. It doesn't exclude criticism or saying "no." It actually refers to making every action, whatever that may be, with the complete intensity of the mind and body.

ANALYZE SUGGESTIONS RECEIVED FROM YOUR ENVIRONMENT

In addition, we must not only reflect upon whether the mind is positive or negative but also consider the nature of our environment. For example, our environment is influenced by the words and actions of other people, by the appearance of our surroundings, and by an almost endless variety of other factors. These factors amount to "suggestions" that we receive from our surroundings and circumstances. Which of these everyday suggestions are positive, and which are negative? By answering this question, we can restructure our surroundings so that our subconscious minds are influenced in a positive way.

Positive elements influence the subconscious, which thereby influences our conscious thoughts and actions. For this reason, a traditional *dojo* (training hall) is clean, uncluttered, bright, orderly, and natural in appearance because these elements affect learning. At the same time, by being aware of the influences in our environment, especially those that we cannot control, we can be unaffected by the negative words, actions, and gestures of others. In this manner, we keep our minds free from negative thoughts. It's for this reason that students practicing in a traditional dojo avoid making negative statements such as, "I can't do that exercise," which not only weakens them, but also has a dispiriting effect on others training in the dojo.

EXAMINE YOUR ATTITUDE TOWARD OTHERS

This is another essential point in the positive use of the mind in Japanese yoga and other Japanese Ways. We must consider the effects of our expressions and actions upon the other members of our dojo (since most of the Ways aren't practiced in isolation). If we speak to people in a discouraging manner, it not only weakens them, but "poisons" our own environment. This can then make us feel less than positive and vigorous. Soon, we may create a "vicious cycle" through our own negative behavior, and in fact this is a frequent cause of lack of accord within a family or even within society as a whole.

In the Japanese Ways, *wa* ("harmony") is essential. Without this quality, a dojo (or even a nation) cannot function effectively. Wa can, at least partially, be cultivated by always using positive, encouraging words when addressing others.

DISCOVER THE PRESENT

Allowing the mind to rest in the present is also essential for a positive mental condition. In feudal-era Japan, the traditional warrior class considered this idea deeply. For a *bushi* (samurai), facing death was an everyday concern. In fact, the bushi's life was likened to the Japanese cherry blossom, which blooms only briefly, displays vibrant color and beauty, and is then scattered by the wind.

The bushi was bound by a strict code of conduct and accountability. In essence, the bushi's main obligations and code of ethics centered on the concept of giving his life in the service of his country, clan, and feudal lord. Adhering to *giri* ("obligation") meant that he could be required to lay down his life, without hesitation, at a moment's notice.

71

As a result, some warriors resolved to live each day as if it were their last. In doing so, according to various accounts, they discovered how to experience life fully without indecision or regret. The bushi's goal wasn't simply to exist, but to live a full and vibrant life.

In short, for the bushi to maintain a positive attitude in the face of possible impending death, he had to learn not to worry about either the past or, especially, the future. This point is also vital for the modern student of Shin-shin-toitsu-do. Basically, if the mind stays in the present, it's impossible to worry. Upon careful consideration, it becomes clear that human beings are capable of worrying only about an event that has already transpired or one that may take place in the future (although the occurrence might have just happened or may be about to happen in the next instant). The present moment contains no time or space for worry.

Retaining our capacity for reason is common sense, but definite conclusions and beliefs keep us from seeing life as it really is at any given moment.

Our past cannot be changed, and to be preoccupied with it is inefficient in time and effort. Likewise, by fretting over the future, we only exhaust ourselves, making us less able to effectively respond when the future is actually upon us. By worrying about a mishap that may or may not take place, we're forced to undergo the event twice—once when imagining it and once again if and when we actually experience it.

By keeping the mind in the present, unless you deliberately want to contemplate the past or future, it's possible to firmly face life without fear. Then, no thoughts of past failures or future problems will exist in the mind, and a truly positive mental state will result—fudoshin, the "immovable mind."

When the mind is in the past or the future, we're not encountering reality. We are, rather, coming face to face with our memories, prejudices, and ingrained beliefs. Clearly, the past no longer exists except in the form of memory, which is highly subjective. The future is also unknown, and any thoughts we have about it are only extrapolations based on the past. Neither the past nor the future has any current basis in reality.

When considering methods of meditation, we may wonder about many things. What is the lineage of a certain teacher? Has he or she experienced enlightenment? What's it like to be one with the universe? In fact, many of us ponder just about everything except *what is*. "What is" equals reality. Why don't we bring the mind into the present to see reality for what it is at that instant? Perhaps because we depend on the writings of others, the words of supposed authorities, ancient documents . . . everything but existence that's right before our eyes. If we had no scriptures, if no sensei, guru, or master were instructing us, then what would we do? How would we proceed if we wished to know the essential nature of the universe and ourselves?

We'd have to begin by deeply acknowledging the fact that we do not know. (This is actually the beginning and the end.) Knowing nothing, having no set conclusions, making no assumptions, we would have to give our full attention to reality as it is at this moment. We would need to enter into the undiscovered. That which is known and discovered is of the past by definition. We're interested in a direct, undiluted experience of the now.

In this immediate perception of the moment, will the undiscovered come to us? Let's find out together.

EXPERIENCE THE UNIVERSAL MIND

The undiscovered is not far away. It's not something to be found eventually. It is contained within what is right in front of us. The essence of reality is being born right now. It has never existed before. Reality is constant creation and destruction, and in this constant change is something unborn and undying, something that cannot be approached through the known or the past. It isn't seen through striving to become something based on ideals stemming from former experiences. It comes to that which is *being*, not striving. In this state of being in the moment, without the known, without knowing at all, with neither past nor future, is a space that is not filled with time. And in this space, the undiscovered and ever-changing moment exists—a moment containing all possibilities, the totality of existence, absolute reality. Reality is now, and in the now, we can experience the true nature of the universe and the universal mind.

The Manifestation of the Universal Mind

The ki of the universe is one and absolute, but its manifestations in our relative world take on various characteristics. While these characteristics are as endless as the number of phenomenon that exist, for the purposes of this discussion we can acknowledge certain categories, realizing that these divisions overlap to some degree and are in some ways artificial. In the case of inanimate objects, such as rocks, we can see the material attribute of ki. In this case, ki manifests itself as form and tangible structure.

We also see shape and form in the plant world, but with an added twist—the ki of instinctive reaction. A plant has form, but more than this, it will automatically bend toward a source of light, displaying an instinct for growth and self-preservation. Rocks don't possess such an attribute, and this is one example of how instinctive reaction separates material ki from the ki of plants.

In the animal kingdom, we see the attributes of both form and instinct, but ki in the animal realm has yet another dimension—emotion. While we could argue as to whether or not plants have feelings, most of us will acknowledge that, at the very least, emotion is more developed and distinguishable in the animal world. It's what separates plants from animals.

And what of the "human animal?" Ki in human form displays structure, instinctive reaction, and emotion, but at around three years of age we start to display the identifying trait of reason. Although certain clever animals show limited reasoning capacity, we still think of this as primarily a human attribute. Human society has gone to great lengths to cultivate this trait, elevating it as the "pinnacle of humanity."

Is this really the case? Without a doubt, reasoning capacity is a distinguishing attribute of humankind. Yet in the rare documented cases of children that have been raised by animals or grown up in an environment largely void of human interaction, they've shown a lack of reasoning ability, functioning on a near animalistic level. So, while the capacity for reason appears to be innate, it must also be developed. In short, it is in many ways an acquired trait.

Moreover, within humanity we see a constant struggle between emotion and reason. One is inborn, while the other is to a large degree cultivated. It's easily possible to envision situations in which both forces are equally compelling. What then?

In India, Nakamura Sensei was presented with a number of questions to ponder. Among them was the question, "What is a human being?" In other words, how is human ki different from the ki of rocks, plants, and animals? (Of course, in an absolute sense, it is the same.)

All creations are one with the universe. Look at the world around you. Can you effectively separate yourself from everything else? After seriously pondering this, most of us rapidly conclude that we cannot. To even make the statement that I exist as a unique entity requires comparison with something else. (If you exist as a distinct being, your distinctiveness is in comparison to other creations. No other creations, no individual you.)

All creations are one with the universe, but only humanity has a mind capable of realizing this fact. In Zen, students are sometimes asked to describe their "original face," the one they possessed before their mother and father were born. Before your ki manifested itself as form, instinctive reaction, emotion, or reason—what existed? Nakamura Sensei pointed to something unborn and thus undying. Something always present, more innate than emotion or reasoning, something waiting to be recognized. He called it uchu-rei—the "universal mind," or "universal spirit."

The universal mind is a mind that is not only one with the universe but also capable of recognizing its own oneness. However, this recognition cannot be confused with the mere attribute of reason. The intellect can't conceive of infinity or eternity, and when we describe the universe and the universal mind, that's what we're talking about. What's more, we need to ask if we can separate the mind that perceives the universe from the universe itself. If we cannot, then my universal mind is your universal mind, which is the universe itself. It is ki, the universal connection. So, while it's possible to read this description and grasp the definition of universal mind, the definition doesn't equal experiencing that universal part of ourselves in such a way that we feel unity with the universe as actual reality. Here's a quick example.

Apollo astronaut Edgar Mitchell was the sixth person to walk on the moon. Despite doctorates in both aeronautics and astronautics, and although he realized on an intellectual and scientific level the interconnection of all living creations, it was only in space, looking back at the earth, that the real meaning of this fact suddenly hit him.

> "Looking at the heavens and planets and Earth and sun and moon and all the heavenly bodies out there, I had an insight that was rather powerful to me, and it was that the story about ourselves as told by science was incomplete and possibly flawed," he said in an interview from his home in Florida. "I remembered in my Ph.D. training that my molecules were prototypes of an ancient generation of stars out there. Instead of it being intellectual knowledge . . . it was suddenly deep and personal. I felt the connection rather than thought of it."[2]

Shin-shin-toitsu-do gives us tools and opportunities to discover the actual nature of the universal mind and the true meaning of being human. Universal mind is an attribute that's more innate than either emotion or reason.

"Emotional baggage," which is carried over from the past, colors our perceptions. Likewise, past conclusions and beliefs, based on reasoning that may or may not have been accurate, also tint our perception of reality. Retaining our capacity for reason is common sense, but definite conclusions and beliefs keep us from seeing life as it really is at any given moment.

Emotional reactions can be unreasonable, and reason can be flawed. It's difficult to have deep confidence in either one, especially when they're often at war with each other. But the universal mind exists in the instant, in a moment beyond time, and it sees the universe as it literally is. It's the universe perceiving itself. It is, moreover, something we can have absolute confidence in, and with that confidence, we can maintain a genuinely positive attitude.

The Transformation Potential

Humankind has accumulated generation upon generation of knowledge, the culmination of which is the vast and useful technological array we see everywhere in modern society. Despite this great accumulation of knowledge and technology, we still suffer from starvation and war. The difference between the past and the present is the difference between throwing rocks and shooting missiles. We are still in conflict. Suffering on a fundamental level hasn't ceased. But we nevertheless persist in the notion that if we just amass a bit more knowledge, we'll all be o.k. Maybe a new philosophy will do the trick, or a new system of government. But all of this has been tried many times.

Knowledge builds on the past and has its place. Wisdom is beyond time. It's the direct perception of reality as it is. And in this direct seeing of *what is* lies the potential of transformation—a transformation that is not merely a redecoration of the past but a transformation of humanity that embodies the eternally new.

Jiko Anji: Nakamura Tempu Sensei's Method of Autosuggestion

Most of us have heard of the distinction between the conscious and subconscious aspects of the mind. While we may be able to generally define the conscious and subconscious, are we capable of making practical use of this information?

Nakamura Sensei was one of Japan's earliest scholars of Western psychology. He discovered the following unique method for altering the subconscious mind while living in the Himalayas and, owing to his interest in psychology, explained it in psychological terms that virtually anyone can easily understand.

> We think and feel in the field of real consciousness, but the materials for our thinking and feeling are stored and preserved in the field of subconsciousness.
>
> From our babyhood, through education by parents and other relatives, teachers, friends and by ourselves, the materials in the field of our subconsciousness have been accumulated and preserved; some are of a positive nature and others may be of a not positive nature.[3]

As the conscious mind reacts to stimuli, elements stored in the subconscious arise and combine with our conscious mind to form words and actions. Whether our responses are emotional or logical, we're influenced by the subconscious. In other words, when we see or hear something, our past associations stored in the subconscious often determine the feelings and thoughts we have about it.

In essence, a flow of suggestions and influences streaming from

79

the subconscious constantly affects the conscious mind. At the same time, whatever we think or feel in our normal, waking, conscious state of mind will become yet another element stored in some form in the subconscious. The subconscious and conscious relate by continuously flowing into and influencing each other.

Clearly, the relationship between these two aspects of the mind is interdependent, flowing back and forth in two directions. If materials stored in the subconscious are primarily negative, it becomes difficult to consciously react in a positive way to daily life. Each negative action or expression made during our waking hours in turn is transmitted into the subconscious to be stored as yet another negative element. As a result, a vicious and negative circle is formed, with negative suggestions flowing from the subconscious to the conscious and back again.

However, if a negative cycle can be fostered, so can a positive one. The question is, how can a person who's grown up to be extremely negative break the vicious circle of negative suggestions? Even if a person resolves to be positive his or her attempts are often unsuccessful due to subconscious influences. In short, it's difficult for negative people to give positive suggestions to their subconscious minds. And while it's true that we're surrounded by suggestions coming from our environment and other people, not all suggestions are positive ones. Actually, if our basic orientation is predominantly negative, we have a strong tendency to depress the people around us, who will react by depressing us, and thus form another vicious and negative cycle of information. Moreover, even if we live in an especially positive environment, the suggestions we receive are ultimately not fully within our control.

Jiko anji is a method of changing the subconscious that we can use to shape ourselves directly. (*Jiko* means "self," and *anji* is "suggestion.") It is a means of placing positive elements into the subconscious that has a much greater impact than do ordinary suggestions or affirmations received from the field of waking consciousness. And it's extraordinarily simple, consisting of only three aspects:

meirei anji—"commanding suggestion"
dantei anji—"concluding suggestion"
hanpuku anji—"repeating suggestion"

Meirei anji takes place at a specific moment—the instant before we fall asleep. As we drift into sleep, our waking consciousness is "submerging," which allows the subconscious to come to the forefront. At this moment, we can most effectively make suggestions to the subconscious without going through layers of ordinary consciousness. In other words, whatever happens as we're about to fall asleep penetrates the subconscious mind deeply and directly. Realizing this, Nakamura Sensei taught to keep a small mirror near your bed. Then, when you're about to drift off into sleep, pick up the mirror, look intently at your face for a half minute, and make an audible suggestion to your subconscious. You can create the wording yourself.

Meirei anji is powerful because the directive comes both from you and from the image of you in the mirror. As a result, the effect upon your subconscious is two times greater than a suggestion made without the mirror.

Avoid a "laundry list" of suggestions. One short, succinct suggestion, repeated over a period of months (or until results are achieved) is more effective for altering the subconscious. Using the word "you" as opposed to "I" is also important. By using the mirror, you create the sensation of directly commanding yourself to do something, and saying "you" is more effective in this regard.

Jiko anji alters habits, but the suggestion has to be correctly phrased. If you say to yourself, "You'll never take drugs again," this may not be as effectual as, "You don't need to take drugs," or "You don't like drugs." Each person should find the exact wording that will work best for them and their particular habit. You may in fact take drugs again after using jiko anji because this method only affects the subconscious via repetition over a period of time. It won't necessarily allow you to stop taking drugs overnight, and if your suggestion implies that it will, you'll tend to lose confidence each time you go against the suggestion. But if you simply submit to your subconscious that you don't need, enjoy, or want something, in time you genuinely begin to feel a lack of desire for whatever it is.

Next comes dantei anji, which takes places immediately after waking, when the subconscious is submerging and the conscious mind is becoming dominant. Pick up your mirror and repeat the suggestion from the night before.

Finally, hanpuku anji is the act of repeating the same suggestion to yourself whenever you have a chance during your waking hours. No mirror is needed. Of the three aspects of jiko anji, the commanding suggestion, given just before going to sleep (to be distinguished from going to bed), is most important.

Avoid doing anything other than falling asleep after you make the suggestion to your subconscious. If you watch TV after meirei anji, then David Letterman's monologue could easily be what penetrates your subconscious instead. This is the reason parents often won't allow their children to watch horror movies before sleeping. In many cases, the kids end up dreaming about blood-sucking beasts, only to invade their parents' bedroom during the middle of the night. Our dreams stem from the subconscious, which rises to the forefront during sleep. As a result, if we fall asleep while reading a book or watching television, it's common for the images we've seen or read about to end up in our dreams. (In fact, nightmares and dreams in general stem from the subconscious, therefore by altering the subconscious we can alter the nature of our dreams.)

Habit vs. Immediate Perception

Jiko anji deals with changing subconscious habits, and habit itself is carried over from the past. However, for the mind and body to be one, the mind must function in the present. All genuine learning and growth must likewise take place in the present. If we approach each new situation with a mind that evaluates and reacts based primarily on past beliefs, prejudices, and habits, we fail to encounter the present as it is. We instead see the moment through the eyes of the past, which colors all our perceptions and keeps us caught in the past. This makes it impossible to discover anything truly new.

We must then wonder if we might not be better off eliminating habits altogether instead of changing the subconscious via jiko anji. We could then perhaps experience reality in its true, unconditioned form and see the real nature of existence with a "pure mind." It's only when we drop what we think we know that we can see ourselves and our lives as they are in actuality.

While the elimination of habit seems to make sense from a meditative standpoint, we must still consider the function of memory and habit in daily life. Clearly, we can't forget how to perform basic subtraction and addition. We must retain certain habits even to drive a car. Nevertheless, the moment, which is beyond time, can only be encountered by a mind that's not caught in the past.

The relationship between maintaining useful habits and experiencing actual reality, with a mind that is free and clear of the past, is an extremely complex subject. To explore it fully would add far too many pages to this work. Yet, we cannot completely ignore this topic, and subjects relating to it will be introduced in future chapters. As we practice the forms of meditation featured in this book, we'll have an opportunity to look at ourselves and the nature of existence. We'll also have a chance to perceive the characteristics of habit versus the nature of an unconditioned mind.

For example, in the martial arts it's common to state that techniques must be practiced until they're subconscious habits. The idea is that these martial skills can become a conditioned reflex, allowing the martial artist to react instantly even if attacked by surprise. It is popular for even high-ranking teachers to assert that this is one of the most important goals of practice.

While techniques certainly must be drilled until they become second nature, simply training to make martial techniques into habit isn't effective. Cultivating certain ingrained habits so that we can react without thinking seems logical . . . until we give the subject more thought.

Suppose a person practices a series of potentially lethal movements, which are drilled in response to a grabbing attack, with the goal of cultivating a habit that will emerge automatically when under assault. If this habit were successfully developed, how would it be utilized when grabbed by a friend? If our friend becomes drunk at a party and grabs us without warning, such an automatic and devastating response could get us into deep ethical, as well as legal, trouble.

Some martial arts techniques involve a spinning body motion, which, depending on the art, can range from a spinning kick to a large turning motion leading into a throw. This action will work well in a traditional training hall or on a relatively dry, even surface, but when standing on ice or on wet grass, such an action can result in a total loss of balance. What happens if the martial artist is unexpectedly attacked in the ice and snow? Under such circumstances, a spinning motion, which would emerge as an automatic reflex, is perhaps one of the worst responses. Thus, in the martial arts certain reflexes must be trained, but the mind must still remain in the moment, quickly evaluating what is *really* taking place. To simply rely on habits that have been previously cultivated in prearranged drills in a controlled environment may not be appropriate for actions that are taking place in the present. The present must be seen for what it genuinely is, and then ingrained techniques can be modified or utilized in their original form as is appropriate.

This example stems from one of the traditional Japanese Ways, but it deals with an issue that has very broad implications. We cannot fully and clearly experience life through the veil of habit, by living and reacting on "automatic pilot." At the same time, we cannot function without retaining certain elements as memory and without maintaining certain habits. Bear this point in mind as you continue to explore this book, and see whether you can discover the resolution of this seemingly contradictory aspect of human life by observing yourself in meditation and daily interaction.

PRINCIPLE # 2: USE THE MIND WITH FULL CONCENTRATION

As I've stated before, unless the mind and body work together as a unit, it's difficult to perform at your optimal level. If the mind and body aren't in harmony, we feel at odds with ourselves and are utilizing only partial power. Unless we regard each moment in Shin-shin-toitsu-do training (or everyday life) in a positive way, our minds will refuse to concentrate on activities that, even unconsciously, they don't want to participate in or do not believe they can effectively participate in. Along these lines, without the capacity to fully concentrate the mind on whatever the body is doing, it's impossible to fully maintain coordination. The difference between an unfocused mind and a concentrated mind can be likened to the distinction between a flashlight and a laser beam. Nakamura Tempu Sensei chose to emphasize this point in the second of the Four Basic Principles to Unify Mind and Body.

In Japanese yoga, examples exist of amazing feats and demonstrations of mental and physical prowess, some of which are detailed in this book. These demonstrations and exercises are sometimes considered to be illustrations of the power of ki. And while this description is not necessarily inaccurate, these seemingly superhuman abilities can also be ascribed to the positive and concentrated power of the mind used in conjunction with the body's strength. Therefore, the vigor of ki and its practical application is related to positive thought and concentration. The positive use of the mind unleashes the vibrant power of ki, and the concentrated use of the mind securely directs and focuses ki. It's vital for the student of Shin-shin-toitsu-do to consider what kind of practice will allow him or her to discover *shuchu-ryoku*—the power of concentration.

Experimenting with the Power of Concentration

We can see our power of concentration in its influence on our bodies. Let's try another experiment to discover how the focusing of the mind can be tested through the body. My teacher Hashimoto Sensei and other senior members of Tempu-kai indicate that, like the previous three experiments, Nakamura Tempu Sensei developed the following test of concentration and mental power in the early 1900s. According to Hashimoto Sensei, these four tests of mind/body coordination were frequently utilized to illustrate the Four Basic Principles to Unify Mind and Body in Nakamura Sensei's introductory lectures.

Since Nakamura Sensei's death, these exercises have been incorporated into other Do forms, particularly aikido. This isn't surprising, as he always encouraged his students to use what he taught in all aspects of their lives. Since many Japanese arts value unification of mind and body, teachers of other disciplines found their way to Nakamura Tempu Sensei. In the case of prominent aikido teachers like Abe Tadashi Sensei and Sasaki Masando Sensei (Sasaki Masao), Shin-shin-toitsu-do was especially well-received owing to the friendship between Nakamura Sensei and Ueshiba Morihei Sensei, founder of aikido. Tohei Koichi Sensei, one of the top disciples of both Ueshiba Sensei and Nakamura Sensei, introduced some of Nakamura Sensei's exercises and teachings, such as orenai te and jiko anji, to aikido students and to the public outside of Japan starting in the 1950s. He subsequently formed his own modern, modified system of Shin-shin-toitsu-do and his own version of aikido—Shin-shin-toitsu aikido.

In teaching Shin-shin-toitsu-do, Mr. Nakamura often compared the mind to the lens of a camera. If the camera lens is out of focus or

87

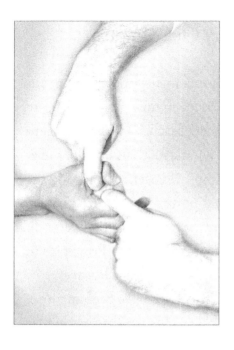

Fig. 4. Experiment Four. Make a ring of your thumb and index finger. A friend inserts each of his index fingers into the ring. As your partner attempts to slowly pull your fingers apart, use the muscle strength of your fingers to try to keep them together. Next, focus your mind on a single thought—your fingers have formed an indestructible ring—and ask your friend to try again. What happens?

smeared, no accurate representation of reality is possible. Using the mind with full attention is similar to functioning with a clean and focused lens. Most people can appreciate the value of a positive attitude and improved concentration, but not everyone has found a means to personally experiment with the nature of concentration. The following exercise gives you an opportunity to do just that.

EXPERIMENT FOUR

Make a ring by joining the fingertips of your thumb and index finger as in Figure 4. Have a friend insert each of his or her index fingers into the ring. One finger hooks around your index finger and the other around your thumb. Your partner, using the strength of both arms, will attempt to slowly pull your fingers apart. Making full use of the muscular strength of your fingers, try to keep them together.

The limited muscular power of the fingers is rarely a match for the force of two arms working together. In most cases, the ring is easily broken. (Be sure to have your friend note how much power was used to pull the fingers apart and at what point they separated.)

Now, imagine your fingers form a ring of solid iron. Since this ring cannot be opened there's no need to excessively tense your fingers, and to do so would actually weaken your unity of mind and body. However, you should press the fingertips together enough so that you have a sensation of firm connection, which will help you to visualize an unbreakable ring.

Focus the mind deeply on a single thought—your fingers have formed an indestructible ring of iron—then ask your friend to try to pull them apart again. Have him or her use the same amount of force as before. What's the result?

Many people find a clear-cut difference between using the limited strength of the body versus the unlimited potential of a concentrated mind that's used in conjunction with the body. Your partner should test you in the same way each time and avoid sudden applications of force so your concentration isn't broken.

Remember that in all mind and body coordination exercises, to make a valid, objective comparison, a similar amount of power should be used every time.

You can also try the following variations of this exercise:

1. Compare tensing your fingers versus visualizing ki flowing around your fingers to form a ring of life energy (instead of imagining a ring of iron).

2. Once you successfully create this ring of ki, have your

friend sustain the pressure for some time. What happens if you're distracted during this period of time? Can you maintain concentration (and the unbreakable ring, which is a reflection of concentration) for longer than a few seconds?

3. Once you can sustain the ring of ki under your friend's ongoing pressure, suddenly think of withdrawing ki from the ring and sucking it back into your arm. What happens?

4. For a more difficult test of concentration, ask your partner to talk while applying pressure, or tap your shoulder then quickly resume the test, or in some other way attempt to distract you during the experiment. If your mind becomes stuck on where you've been tapped or the words being said, what is the effect on the ring? If you note these sensations but continue to focus on an unbreakable ring or a ring of flowing life energy, what takes place?

These experiments give you an opportunity to graphically test the power of concentration as well as observe how it relates to mind and body unification. What is concentration? How is it sustained? Is it necessary to block out distracting thoughts to arrive at concentration, or will another approach work more effectively? Does the concentrated mind affect the body, and if it does, what's the most efficient way to create that effect?

FOUR PRINCIPLES FOR INVESTIGATING CONCENTRATION

1. Concentrate on matters you are familiar with.

2. Concentrate on matters you wish to accomplish in a hurry.

3. Concentrate on matters you believe are uninteresting.

4. Concentrate on matters you believe are of no value.

Many activities, from seated meditation to martial arts, can be used to unlock the power of concentration. Still, it's not only possible to manifest remarkable concentration by engaging in everyday actions, but it is also vital to do so.

When do people lose concentration, and therefore, their awareness of the moment? For most, it's often when they're doing an extremely familiar activity, such as tying their shoes. For example, how many of us can remember which shoe we tied first this morning? As we're cognizant of this sort of "gap" in awareness, we begin to realize clear consciousness and impeccable concentration in daily life. This practice of constant awareness allows the student of Shin-shin-toitsu-do to actualize a matchless state of mind that has no lapses in concentration.

To continue, quite a few people become so preoccupied with the outcome of an action that they cannot focus the mind on the process taking place that instant. This is a problem for novices of Shin-shin-toitsu-do, who are often so concerned with someday acquiring heightened states of calmness or improved health that they don't fully concentrate on the actual learning process taking place in the present. Simply put, they're in such a hurry to become more powerful mentally and physically that they fail to deeply concentrate on their actions at the moment. In essence then, when we're trying to complete matters in a hurry, we tend to lose concentration. This is not to suggest that it's impossible to act quickly and still concentrate, but rather that we should make sure that we're actually concentrating when hurrying.

Many people also "switch off their concentration" whenever they participate in some activity that they believe is uninteresting. For example, beginning students of most Japanese arts, including Shin-shin-toitsu-do, frequently struggle with the seemingly endless repetitions of basic techniques required by their sensei. What these novices fail to realize is that the real essence of these arts lies in learning their rudiments, which must be drilled continuously to become automatic reactions. Their seniors usually have no problem practicing basic movements repeatedly because they're constantly analyzing and refining numerous minute aspects of these proven fundamentals. What's boring for one person can be fascinating for another.

Therefore, whether or not we can concentrate is at least partially determined by whether or not we have a positive attitude. Even if nothing of interest can be found in a certain activity, it's still possible to use it as an interesting test or exercise to improve one's concentration.

Making sure we concentrate on activities that we think are of no value also relates to developing dynamic powers of concentration, and what we consider to be worthless is relative. In fact, by really paying attention to certain activities, it's frequently possible to discover value where we imagined there was none. It is particularly important for novices in Shin-shin-toitsu-do to realize that this art is not based on short-term gratification, and that the true value of many aspects of practice becomes apparent only after innumerable repetitions.

Rather than simply memorizing the above list of four principles for investigating concentration, try actually experimenting with them. For instance, for one day make a point of noticing what your mental reaction is to activities with which you're familiar. Where does this reaction come from? What does it mean in terms of concentration? In fact, what *is* concentration—not in theory or by definition, but in real life? Think of the above list as four different occasions to discover the genuine nature of a concentrated mind for yourself.

Recent data in experimental psychology indicate that the more vigorously and attentively we use our minds, the less fatigued we become on both mental and physical levels. Bearing this in mind, it would seem logical to adopt the bushi's philosophy of performing each action in life as if it were the first time and as if it might be the last. Using Shin-shin-toitsu-do as a tangible proof of the ability to unrelentingly use the mind in a positive and concentrated manner, it's possible to vitally transform one's life. In this way, it becomes natural to throw 100 percent of ourselves into each moment, pouring ki into every second of life, becoming fully alive—actually living as opposed to merely existing.

The Hara

It's clear that if we use the mind attentively, mental power is increased, and if we concentrate the mind in the moment, it is easier to coordinate mind and body. But in terms of mind and body unity, is there something we can concentrate on that will reliably aid us in discovering this state of coordination?

In Japan, and to some degree other Asian countries, people have historically focused mental strength in the *hara* (abdomen) as a way of realizing their full potential. Japan has traditionally viewed the hara as the vital center of humanity in a manner not dissimilar to the Western view of the heart or brain. I once read that years ago Japanese children were asked to point to the origin of thoughts and feelings. They inevitably pointed toward the abdominal region. When the same question was asked of American children, most pointed at their heads or hearts. Likewise, Japan and the West have commonly held differing views of what is physical power or physical health, with Japan emphasizing the strength of the waist and lower body and Western people admiring upper body power. (Consider the ideal of the sumo wrestler versus the V-shaped Western bodybuilder with a narrow waist and broad shoulders.)

However, East and West also hold similar viewpoints regarding the hara, and we're perhaps not as dissimilar as some might imagine. For instance, *hara ga nai hito* describes a cowardly person, "a person with no hara." Sounds similar to our saying that so-and-so "has no guts," doesn't it? We'll be exploring further how the hara relates to mind and body coordination, but for now, realize that the weight of the upper body reaches its highest point of density below the navel, and this area corresponds to the correct center of gravity and balance for the body. If we focus the mind at this point on the front surface of the lower abdomen about four finger widths below the navel, we're joining the mind and body in the same place and at the same time. Since the body only exists in the present moment, by calming the mind at this spot in the hara, we're bringing the mind into the present as well. In short, we've unified the mind and body.

To concentrate ki, or physical and mental power, in the hara has a long tradition in Asia, and Japanese yoga utilizes this point as a means not only of coordinating the mind and body, but also for realizing mind-body stability and restoring mental composure. Calming the mind in the lower abdomen can help in everything from achieving better balance in sports to stabilizing the mind before a job interview. However, the validity of this statement can only be evaluated via actual practice. Try experimenting with concentrating the mind at this apex. We'll discuss how the hara relates to posture and physical movement in the following chapters, and you'll read about the hara in various Shin-shin-toitsu-do exercises as well.

SHIN, MI: *"body,"* painted in the semicursive gyosho style of Kobara Ranseki Sensei. Despite the fact that the principles of the mind feature first and foremost in Nakamura Sensei's methodology of mind and body coordination, an understanding of how to use the body naturally is essential in Japanese yoga. A tense, off-balance, and unhealthy body cannot respond effectively to the commands of even the most concentrated mind.

Chapter 4

PRINCIPLES
OF THE BODY

It's clear that in Shin-shin-toitsu-do, as well as in life, the mind influences and controls the body. It is equally apparent that a positive, focused mind has a stronger and more positive effect on the body. Nevertheless, unless the body is in its right, natural, and optimal state, it will often fail to quickly, correctly, and competently react to the commands of even the most concentrated mind. The innate harmony that exists between mind and body is one of the secrets behind the amazing power of Shin-shin-toitsu-do, which is weakened by an inefficient use of the body. Our bodies must be strong, relaxed, and healthy to respond to our minds' commands. Let's explore together the vital role of the body in Japanese yoga.

PRINCIPLE #3: USE THE BODY NATURALLY

As human beings, we're born, live, and die as part of nature. This is fairly obvious, but many of us fall short of considering its real meaning as well as how it relates directly to our lives. (Perhaps the very fact that nature completely engulfs us makes us all the more unaware of nature itself.) And simply being part of nature is no guarantee that we'll act as if we're part of nature. Plants or animals rarely behave in an unnatural manner that's contrary to their true makeup. Human beings are also natural beings, but at the same time, we're conscious entities. We therefore have free will and must make the choice not merely to be part of nature, but also to follow faithfully the "laws of nature." (This is the third of the Four Basic Principles to Unify Mind and Body.)

For instance, animals eat when they're hungry and sleep when they're drowsy. This was Nakamura Sensei's advice as well. But such common sense isn't so common. People regularly eat needlessly because they're bored, nervous, or greedy. Other individuals may refuse to eat when they're hungry due to self-consciousness about their appearance. Still others eat unconsciously and without gratitude to the plants and animals that are sacrificed so that they may live.

One aspect of obeying the laws of nature is to simply consume food when we're hungry and to observe ourselves in the moment, in a state free of preconceptions, so as to see our true reactions toward eating. To say that we should be grateful to nature for our food (and not waste it) makes sense, but people still fail to heed this counsel. If this advice is seen as mere theory, it has little impact on us. Why endorse something we don't live?

Many of us advocate what sounds good, what other people believe, how we were raised, or what we'd like to believe. But none of this has anything to do with *what we really are* and *how we actually feel*—what we know firsthand.

We naturally want to be good people, but on what shall we base this "goodness?" Should it be centered in reality? Or should it be based on what we've been told we should be but have never actually experienced for ourselves? The latter leads to burying what *we are* beneath what *we would like to be*. And in many cases, what we would like to be stems from what we believe we should be or what others have told us to become. All of which is supposition, and all of which covers up *what is*. The thought of "becoming good or better" only serves to put matters on hold indefinitely. What are we now? What's the nature of life at the same instant? Right now?

Genuine goodness isn't discovered through postponement but must exist now or not at all. It cannot be based on *what is not*. We must find it in *what is* and what we truly see.

How many of us would take a meat cleaver in our right hand and chop off our left hand? Perhaps only the insane. Despite the fact that the two hands are separate from each other, and even opposite in character, we realize right down to our bones that they're part of a single, larger entity. To harm one is to harm the other. But how many people who state that we're all one with the universe can do so with the same sense of authentic conviction? (I'm not suggesting that oneness with the universe is impossible or that compassion for all creations is not significant. However, I want to make it clear that such harmony and love must be found directly in reality as opposed to being the product of mere sentiment, wishful thinking, or abstract philosophy.) In fact, is conviction necessary when the truth is seen as true by our whole being?

As you practice meditation, you have a chance to look for the

> *Genuine goodness isn't discovered through postponement but must exist now or not at all. It cannot be based on what is not. We must find it in what is and what we truly see.*

dividing line between the meditator and the universe that surrounds him or her. Can this line be found? Is the person that meditates upon the universe separate from the object of meditation? Can we have one without the other? Can we ultimately divide the eater from that which is eaten?

When humanity's absolute unity with all creations is seen as first-hand reality, love manifests itself as genuine reality—then eating with gratitude is natural. With this state of gratitude comes a truly positive attitude toward eating (especially if we eat when we're really hungry, when everything tastes pretty good). Gratitude, like deep sleep, cannot be forced or faked.*

---

* Because the mind controls the body, a positive attitude even affects our digestion in a positive way. Yet philosophizing about this is unproductive and only distracts us from the genuine task at hand of discovering our actual nature and that of the universe.

In fact, when it comes to sleeping, the more we try to sleep, the more we keep ourselves awake. By entering into a state of "doing nothing," sleep happens easily. In the following chapters on meditation, we'll look at doing nothing (mui in Japanese) and its relationship to relaxation. In essence, worrying about sleeping makes sleep impossible. And since the mind affects the body, worrying excessively about what to eat actually has a detrimental effect on our health.

Of course, we should eat a balanced diet, and common sense tells us to chew food well, which aids in digestion and the natural production of saliva. Likewise, we should make sure we drink enough, replacing lost water promptly. And many people have heard of the dangers of eating too much meat, sugar, salt, and fat. Fruits, vegetables, and grains are healthy foods. But diet still varies according to the person and numerous other factors. Age, sex, race, body type, physical condition, and even location play a role in what we should eat. Can we really say, for example, that a Brazilian male living in a hot climate, age 65, sedentary, and overweight should follow the same diet as an active, slender 18-year-old Asian girl living in Alaska?

While general, common sense principles of diet may pertain, the specifics of what to eat will vary. So why not let people discover the right personal diet for themselves? If the mind rests calmly in the present, in a condition that's free from preconceived ideas, is it possible to notice what does and doesn't work well for your body? Anything less is to see ourselves and nature through the eyes of others, who don't ultimately know us. And can we genuinely have confidence in what's copied or memorized as opposed to that which we've directly seen for ourselves? Without this confidence, relaxation is difficult.

And in many ways, to relax and follow our true character is to be in harmony with nature.

Positive Relaxation

Relaxation is essential for mastering Shin-shin-toitsu-do, and while many teachers of the yoga recognize this, they're sometimes at a loss as to how they should teach it. But without the maintenance of a relaxed condition, it's difficult to achieve stability and power in any form of yoga.

Even if we were to memorize this book, this would have little meaning if we were incapacitated by stress-related ailments such as high blood pressure or chronic ulcers that would indicate that we've failed to derive all of the potential benefits from Shin-shin-toitsu-do. Ultimately, Shin-shin-toitsu-do is a tool to help us function freely in life, which means avoiding physical and mental illnesses, including stress-related afflictions. (Note that several leading figures in Shin-shin-toitsu-do history, including Nakamura Tempu Sensei, lived to a ripe old age.) Many people feel that they're "attacked" by stress on a daily basis, and Shin-shin-toitsu-do (when it's correctly practiced) should help us discover functional relaxation that can be carried into everyday affairs.

In fact, if the Shin-shin-toitsu-do practitioner isn't able to remain composed even during extreme stress, it is doubtful that he or she will arrive at freedom of expression in any aspect of life. As we've learned in previous chapters, the mind moves the body, while the body acts as a reflection of the mind. And as a result, if we "freeze" mentally in a traumatic situation, we "freeze" physically as well, and we'll be unable to execute any effective action.

We may realize this, but few seem capable of actually achieving relaxation in action. Is relaxation unnatural or especially difficult? Or does this difficulty often arise from certain mistaken beliefs and incorrect habits (such as sitting or standing with the shoulders slightly raised, which produces tension, stiff shoulders, and headaches instead of relaxing and letting the shoulders fall into their proper place naturally)?

Instead of attempting to guess an answer, let's began by observing others and ourselves. Many people either consciously or unconsciously believe that relaxation is comfortable but also weak. At the least, they seem to feel that relaxation doesn't allow a person to manifest great physical power. Some people, in addition, may feel that when they're relaxed, they're not working hard or doing their best.

Once this idea becomes part of the subconscious, it influences all conscious actions. Therefore, in an emergency or other stressful situation, we find ourselves unable to relax even if we want to. One fundamental tenet of Shin-shin-toitsu-do holds that as we deliberately and consciously discover relaxation and calmness under duress in practice, we also cultivate the ability to relax under stress as a subconscious state, which undeniably affects our daily lives. (Remaining composed while practicing orenai te, for example, gives us an opportunity to learn how to deal with stress. It also illustrates how genuine relaxation is anything but weak.)

Plants or animals rarely behave in an unnatural manner that's contrary to their true makeup. Human beings are also natural beings, but at the same time, we're conscious entities. We therefore have free will and must make the choice not merely to be part of nature, but also to follow faithfully the "laws of nature."

Realize that both positive and negative forms of relaxation are also possible. For many individuals, the distinction between the two isn't clear. Weakness and softness of body aren't the same thing. Relaxation and slackness again are not the same. Real relaxation is filled with ki; limpness is similar to losing ki. Along the same lines, is resignation the same as acceptance? Is choosing not to fight the same as giving up? And what's the relationship between true relaxation, acceptance, and non-dissension? Guessing answers to such questions is not necessary. Engage in the previous experiments such as orenai te, observe yourself as you practice the upcoming exercises, and discover directly the actual nature of relaxation in action.

Positive relaxation indicates a dynamic posture in which the mind and body are in harmony. When mind and body function as a single unit, we're in our most natural and relaxed state, but we're also filled with power. Negative relaxation is to relax without this state of harmony. It's a state of physical and mental "limpness" that amounts to surrendering vigor, while positive relaxation is filled with vitality but free from unnecessary tension.

In Shin-shin-toitsu-do, and in everyday life, an "alive" condition that's balanced between tension and collapse is needed. Fundamentally, relaxation and collapse aren't the same, and each produces different results in terms of mind-body unity and the flow of ki.

Let the Body Settle into Its Natural Posture

One of nature's laws is gravity. The weight of all objects, including the human body, is naturally disposed to settle downward. Upon reflection, this simple observation has the potential to produce profound changes in the way we function in life.

Because everything in nature tends to settle or fall downward, relaxing and harmonizing with nature requires allowing the weight of the body to settle downward in a natural and relaxed way. Any object such as the human body has a center of gravity. A stable and therefore "calm" object's center of gravity has settled internally to a relatively low point, while an unstable object has a higher center of gravity.

If we adopt a fully erect, aligned posture that doesn't sag or cause us to slump, our upper body's weight settles at a point below the navel. This spot equals our physical center of gravity and center of balance—our hara.

In Japan, people have believed that to manifest our greatest strength, we must focus power in the abdomen. Nakamura Sensei taught the same. But this is a rather general statement. More specifically, we must focus the mind's power and concentration in the *tanden* (lower abdomen). Even more specifically, we need to concentrate energy at a point or natural center in the tanden. This point is sometimes thought to be three *sun* (an ancient Japanese measurement) below the navel (about 3.6 inches). For Westerners (and larger Japanese), about four finger widths below the navel is a good place to start.*

If we adopt an erect, relaxed posture, the center of gravity settles at a spot on the front surface of the lower abdomen that corresponds to the center of balance. By dropping concentration to this point, it's possible to powerfully mesh together the mind and body, achieving a positive form of relaxation. Harmony of mind and body, in turn, results in an exceptionally stable posture and vital psychophysical condition.

---

* The exact location will vary according to the size of the person. Therefore, instead of saying that the correct center of concentration is exactly 4 inches below the navel, it may be more effective to use the measurement of your fingers. A smaller person will have smaller fingers, and a larger individual's fingers are usually wider. In other words, while a measurement of 4 inches might be effective for the average adult, it will be too low on a small child and perhaps not low enough on a pro basketball player.

This posture and attitude is extremely powerful, and even when forcefully tested by our practice partners in Shin-shin-toitsu-do, it's stable to the point of being seemingly immovable. However, in this state, we are also capable of quick reaction and fluid movement. By repeatedly studying through Shin-shin-toitsu-do the differences between limpness, relaxation, and tension, it is possible to impress these vital distinctions upon the subconscious and create a functional or "positive" relaxation. In this way, we can achieve a relaxed but dynamic state in which we're ready to calmly meet any emergency or stressful situation.

Let's discover if by being aware of posture, it's possible to arrive at functional relaxation, which due to its potent and dynamic nature, can be utilized and maintained even under extreme stress. If we're going to experiment with this idea, we want to avoid a posture that's sagging and appears small, collapsed, or withdrawn. We also want to avoid adopting an overly erect, rigid stance. Why?

Look at people who use their bodies with great efficiency and coordination in physical activities requiring quickness and mobility. For instance, we don't often see top athletes in basketball, skiing, tennis, judo, and kendo initially take up a stiff, tense posture because quick movement from such a position is difficult. Although it may be possible to perform from an artificial, rigid stance under prearranged circumstances, it's generally incompatible with free and spontaneous encounters. Would this fact also hold true in non-athletic activities? To find out, experiment with a posture that is completely erect and relaxed without becoming rigid—a "large presence." This is the posture of mind and body unification.

When we use Shin-shin-toitsu-do to test and discover how to remain relaxed under pressure, it becomes more than a mere health exercise and can be thought of as dynamic meditation that embodies real and unshakable calmness. Ultimately, in Shin-shin-toitsu-do and in daily life, tranquility is strength.

Kumbhaka

It's possible to focus the mind at the hara to calm ourselves, but if the nervous system is under great stress, this is easier said than done. Nakamura Sensei offered to the public his own version of a special method of regulating the nervous system and concentrating ki in the hara that he learned in India. It is called *kumbhaka*.

In Nakamura Sensei's methodology, kumbhaka refers to two things: a posture of self-harmony that settles the body's weight in the lower abdomen, unites mind and body, and regulates the autonomic nervous system; and a breathing method to focus ki at the hara even during moments of serious stress. Let's first consider the posture of kumbhaka.

Posture relates to the human nervous system. In some people, the nervous system has become hypersensitive, so that even a small stimulus is felt to be much larger than it is in reality. Other individuals' nervous systems may have been dulled, and as a result, any stimulus appears muted in intensity to them. Basically, they exhibit under-reaction, slow reaction, or no reaction.

Through a correct, natural posture and the coordination of mind and body, it's possible to maintain the autonomic nervous system in a balanced, ordered condition. Arriving at kumbhaka posture is essential in Japanese yoga, so Nakamura Sensei reduced its essentials down to just three points:

1. Relax and drop the shoulders.

2. Focus power at a point in the lower abdomen.

3. Do not let any part of the body, including the anus, fall limp.

While these points are easy to read, real understanding of exactly what Nakamura Sensei meant by them is another matter. Not all of his students agree on their interpretation. Some disciples also state that his explanation of how to perform kumbhaka changed shortly before he passed away, only to be changed back by the leaders of the organization he left behind. The following explanation is based on what I've absorbed from practicing with direct pupils of Nakamura Sensei and reflects my current understanding of kumbhaka (or, in Japan, *kunbahaka*).

The innate harmony that exists between mind and body is one of the secrets behind the amazing power of Shin-shin-toitsu-do, which is weakened by an inefficient use of the body. Our bodies must be strong, relaxed, and healthy to respond to our minds' commands.

RELAX THE SHOULDERS

Relaxing the shoulders is vital for relaxation in general. However, owing to the effects of gravity, relaxation is problematic unless we let the shoulders remain in their natural place. Let the shoulders drop, or settle in harmony with gravity, into their most comfortable position. It isn't too difficult to do this for a moment, but to sustain this condition unconsciously in our lives is another matter. We raise our shoulders unnaturally when we lean on a desk or hold the telephone between our shoulders and ears, when we are shocked by a loud noise, and who knows how many other times throughout the day. And the unsettling of the shoulders doesn't have to be large to produce anxiety, stiff necks, and headaches. Just slightly raising them will create tension, and this tension throws the nervous system out of balance.

When do we raise the shoulders in daily life? What are we feeling at that moment and leading up to that moment? Remembering that the body reflects the mind, and that the raising of the shoulders not only creates tension but also is a physical manifestation of psychological tension itself, what are the roots of this tension? Bringing the mind into the moment, let's observe ourselves in a state free of preconceived ideas or beliefs. Don't guess at these questions. Observe yourself in relationship to others and the universe.

Dropping the shoulders is easy. Keeping them down is a whole different ballgame. Why do they sometimes rise again? In other words, once we relax, why does tension return, and what is its origin?

FOCUS POWER IN THE LOWER ABDOMEN

If we relax the upper body, its weight settles downward to a point below the navel. Observing this leads to Nakamura Tempu Sensei's second principle for kumbhaka. Exactly how to put power into the lower abdomen is what must be discovered. As noted previously, this can perhaps be best accomplished by releasing tension from the body, letting the body's weight drop to the hara by responding to gravity, and focusing attention and ki about four finger widths below the navel. Concentrating the mind at this point is also useful for making sure the body's center of gravity is in the lower torso.

Using this method, it's possible to concentrate psychophysical force in the hara. Once the mind grows calm at this point, the body naturally relaxes, and the weight of the upper body reacts to relaxation and follows the mind's movement downward. This produces a posture that's exceptionally stable yet capable of quick reaction. It's an unwavering structure that is bottom-heavy as opposed to top-heavy.

Once we get the feeling of unifying the mind and body by centering ourselves in the hara, it isn't necessary to continue to focus the mind at this point. From this stage, we can carry the feeling and power of mind and body unity into daily affairs by just behaving naturally and going about our business. If we become tense, or in some way lose the state of harmony, we only need to recenter ourselves in the hara.

All of nature exists in a condition of flux. The extraordinary benefits of Shin-shin-toitsu-do lie in lifelong participation. If we cease to practice, no matter how long we've been studying or how talented we are, our health and ability suffer.

DO NOT LET YOUR BODY GO LIMP

Relaxation can be mistaken for "collapsation," which is ineffective for mind-body coordination and regulating the nervous system. To create a sense of postural balance, Nakamura Sensei indicated that the body's muscles, including the sphincter muscles of the anus, shouldn't fall limp. His reason for offering this advice has roots in certain health systems of India, where he encountered the idea, and also in some Japanese methods that have a somewhat parallel tradition. Briefly stated, the fundamental concept is that the constricting power of the anus has a correlation to human life power.

Some books on Hatha yoga describe an anal *bandha*, or "lock." Another example can be found in the ancient Japanese art of resuscitation called *kappo*. Aspects of this art can be used to revive a person whose breathing has stopped because of drowning or strangulation.

In old Japan, if someone pulled from a river had stopped breathing, the local kappo expert was quickly summoned. While it wasn't uncommon for such healers to resuscitate people who'd been unconscious in the water for a number of minutes, obviously revival was not possible in every case. To determine if there was any point in attempting kappo, some experts would insert a finger into the victim's anus. If no muscle resistance or reaction were felt, the situation would be deemed hopeless, as the nervous system no longer responded to external stimulus. On the other hand, if resistance could be felt, or if the muscles weren't totally flaccid, then kappo was attempted, with frequently effective results. This is an example of how some Japanese healing arts have viewed the correlation between the constricting strength of the anus and human life power.

Correct coordination of mind and body requires an equivalently correct posture. This posture is one in which every part of the body, inside and out, is "knitted together," with all of the body's muscles working together as a unit. It is, as previously noted, a posture that's neither tense nor limp nor disconnected—and this lack of slackness extends to even the body's internal structure.

Fig. 5. Sit in a slumped position and see how difficult it is to unify mind and body.

Practicing Kumbhaka

Try sitting slumped over as in Figure 5. Notice the overall external muscular sensation, and note in particular the slack feeling in the buttocks and anus. In such a position, it's difficult to unify mind and body because we aren't in a state of functional relaxation. Moreover, the body's weight has shifted away from its natural center in the lower abdomen and instead moved toward the buttocks.

Fig. 6. Now, straighten your lower back and restore your natural forward lumbar curve. Your muscles should feel neither tense nor slack.

Now, very slowly and with full consciousness, gradually straighten your lower back so that you restore your natural forward lumbar curve. As you correct your posture, notice how the muscles slightly tighten in the buttocks and sphincter areas. You'll also feel a delicate constriction of the muscles in the lower back, waist, and abdominal areas. The feeling is subtle—certainly not as crude as tightly constricting the anus or deliberately hardening the hara—and you may need to slowly try this experiment several times to catch on to the sensation being described (Figure 6).

You can arrive at a condition in which the muscles are neither tense nor slack by using an expansive posture that feels light. When sitting down, for instance, try setting yourself down lightly in your chair, almost as if your rear end were sore. I think you'll find the same state of positive relaxation as before. In contrast, see what happens to the appearance of your posture, and the feeling in the body's muscles, when you plop down heavily. Sitting, standing, walking, and lying down buoyantly, as if you're floating in the center of the cosmos, is an ideal way of fulfilling the third principle of kumbhaka.

Kumbhaka Breathing

I'd describe the posture of kumbhaka as one in which we drop the shoulders, settling our body's weight and our mind's power into a natural center in the lower abdomen while maintaining an erect, light carriage. Such a position balances and maintains order in the nervous system, allowing us to remain composed in daily living. But what if this composure is lost and repeated attempts to calm the mind in the hara fail to produce calmness? To deal with this situation, Nakamura Sensei introduced kumbhaka breathing.

What's the condition of your breathing when you're sleeping, when you first wake up, or when you're deeply relaxed? And what does your breathing become like when you're scared or angry? Deep and slow breathing has been associated with calmness and meditation. Rapid, shallow respiration is commonly thought to be a sign of mental and physical disturbance. Kumbhaka breathing involves a process of deep, slow breathing, including the retention of breath, which makes use of our full lung capacity. (Few people use their lungs fully and efficiently, and as a result, their health suffers.) Oxygen in general has a calming effect on the body.

What follows is a simplified version of Nakamura Sensei's kumbhaka breathing that we're practicing at the Sennin Foundation Center for Japanese Cultural Arts, and it should be easy for the average person to utilize. We can use it in any position and at any time, but it's important to embody the three postural points.

While it's possible to perform kumbhaka by breathing via the mouth, for many of us it is easiest and most discreet to breathe in and out through the nose. Inhale as slowly, deeply, and calmly as possible—as if you were filling your whole body, starting at your toes, with air. As you inhale, mentally aim the air toward your hara. Make absolutely certain that your shoulders do not rise. Then hold your breath for several seconds without straining. Have the sensation of dropping all of the air toward your lower abdomen, and focus your ki in the hara. This is kumbhaka.

In Shin-shin-toitsu-do, we have a chance to rest peacefully in the present, and in our timeless observation of the moment, we may realize a condition transcending fear and duality . . . a state that's both eternal and infinite.

Because of the relaxed visualization taking place (mentally aiming air toward the hara), you'll efficiently breathe from the diaphragm as opposed to the top of your lungs. When you visualize retaining your breath in the lower abdomen, the downward pressure of the diaphragm creates a feeling of relaxed power in the hara. This visceral sensation makes it easier to focus ki below the navel. In this way, you can more effectively calm your mind in the hara. So that a downward movement of the diaphragm is produced, holding the breath is the most important moment in kumbhaka breathing.

Now, exhale slowly, calmly, and fully. The exhalation tends to be a bit longer and more powerful than the inhalation. Pause slightly at the bottom of your breath. One or two repetitions of this breathing cycle should do the trick.

Right after exhaling and at the conclusion of inhaling, power is focused below the navel and at the anus. This should take place naturally and without deliberate force. Some of Nakamura Sensei's students rather emphatically push the hara in and out as they breathe, while strenuously tightening the hara and anus. But based on my conversations with direct students of Nakamura Sensei and on photos and videotapes of him, it doesn't seem to me that Nakamura Sensei practiced this way. His actions were natural and relaxed.

It's the combination of increased oxygen intake and downward pressure of the diaphragm toward the hara that makes this breathing method an easy way to relax the body and calm the mind even in the middle of great stress. During WWII, a number of Nakamura Tempu Sensei's students avoided death by using this kumbhaka posture and breathing to maintain order in their nervous systems during severe bombing raids. Quite a few of these former soldiers report comrades dying from shock due to the overwhelming stimulus of exploding bombs, while they were relatively unaffected.

Hatha yoga teacher Howard Kent has written:

By means of quiet intuition and experimentation, yogis

realized a long time ago that the control of breathing involves not only inhalation and exhalation, but also the way in which the breath is retained. They called the stopping of the breath *kumbhaka* . . .

When something happens suddenly, causing the necessity of making an instant decision, you stop breathing immediately. If you are driving your car and someone steps out in front of you, you hold your breath without a fraction of a delay. This is because this concentrates the mind totally for a short period while you brake, swerve, or take any other action.[4]

The posture of kumbhaka is maintained during all of the exercises outlined in this book. Be sure to research its relationship to daily life as well. Correct posture is the key to eliminating backaches, stiff shoulders, and tension. It makes for a longer, more comfortable existence.

PRINCIPLE #4: TRAIN THE BODY GRADUALLY, SYSTEMATICALLY, AND CONTINUOUSLY

Shin-shin-toitsu-do practice is a form of physical training, and it is essential that training in this art be conducted in a natural manner. Without naturalness in the way we exercise, it's inevitable that we'll sustain physical injury, making continuing practice difficult. Nakamura Tempu Sensei's fourth principle gives us a chance to reflect on what is, and is not, natural in terms of exercising the body.

To avoid injury, practice gradually. As numerous physicians and sports specialists will confirm, the best way of "warming up" for any physical activity is to gently perform the movements of the activity itself. Students should make a point of practicing the physical aspects of Japanese yoga more softly at the beginning, gradually increasing intensity with each repetition. We not only progress by degrees from day to day, but also from moment to moment within a given exercise. How gradually an individual builds up to practicing with greater vigor is

When we use Shin-shin-toitsu-do to test and discover how to remain relaxed under pressure, it becomes more than a mere health exercise and can be thought of as dynamic meditation that embodies real and unshakable calmness.

determined by age and physical condition. It's fully possible for older individuals who are serious and sincere to practice Japanese yoga—providing they add to the intensity of their practice progressively.

It's also necessary to train the mind and body in a systematic, regular manner. Practicing the physical aspects of Shin-shin-toitsu-do sporadically isn't only less effective but also potentially dangerous if carried too far. This is, of course, true for any form of exercise. Placing sudden demands on a body that may have fallen out of condition is never a good idea. Thus, it's more effective to exercise a moderate amount on a frequent basis than to practice a great deal every once in awhile.

Remember as well that the mind and body are in a constant state of change, rarely remaining the same for long. Likewise, all of nature exists in a condition of flux. The extraordinary benefits of Shin-shin-toitsu-do lie in lifelong participation. If we cease to practice, no matter how long we've been studying or how talented we are, our health and ability suffer. In other words, Japanese yoga training is valuable only as long as we are in some way engaging in it.

As an example, occasionally students of Shin-shin-toitsu-do and other Japanese Do forms wonder if the large amount of time they put into their practice is worth what they're "getting out of it." While this seems to be a reasonable question, it in fact reveals a fundamental failure to understand Japanese cultural arts, which is sadly not uncommon. In essence, the time we put into practicing an art *is* what we're getting out of it. It's the *process of participation* that's truly valuable, not some eventual goal or byproduct of participation.

All of life truly exists only at this instant. The past and the future reside merely in thought as self-created, artificial realities. In Shin-shin-toitsu-do, we have a chance to rest peacefully in the present, and in our timeless observation of the moment, we may realize a condition transcending fear and duality . . . a state that's both eternal and infinite.

In a sense, the practice is the goal—time and thoughts of eventual progress need not enter into the equation. Consequently, practicing Shin-shin-toitsu-do with genuine awareness is to sense the exceptional benefits of the practice itself.

I occasionally meet individuals who inform me that they're teachers of some form of yoga. However, during the conversation, it sometimes becomes clear that they haven't engaged in any aspect of their art for many years. Rather than saying they *are* teachers, it would probably be more accurate to state that they *were* teachers, because it's usually possible to participate in yoga and meditation in some way (for example, through teaching, writing, modified training regimes, etc.) if we really wish to do so. In fact, through gradual, regular, and systematic Shin-shin-toitsu-do training, it's possible to continue to develop as we age since the art doesn't require great physical strength and amounts to a never-ending, moving meditation.

Nakamura Tempu Sensei and his student Hashimoto Tetsuichi Sensei have indicated that ongoing, systematic training in Shin-shin-toitsu-do ultimately consists of only three simple and general elements:

1. Training to reveal the nature of positivity.

2. Reformation of the subconscious.

3. Regulating and maintaining a balanced condition in the nervous system.[5]

The Four Basic Principles to Unify Mind and Body, which include important subprinciples such as projecting ki outward, centering in the lower abdomen, relaxing in a positive way, and allowing body weight to gravitate, can be utilized by virtually anyone of any age, culture, or gender. These principles, along with methods like jiko anji and kumbhaka breathing, all relate to Nakamura Sensei's three central pillars of Shin-shin-toitsu-do training. The following chapters cover additional techniques that help make Shin-shin-toitsu-do a profound art of holistic health maintenance, personal transformation, and self-realization.

SHINNYO: "absolute reality, the absolute," painted in the semicursive gyosho style of the famed calligrapher Ogishi. In genuine meditation, the mind is like a mirror that reflects reality as it truly is. Yet the mirror doesn't cling to any image. If it did, the next reflection would have the first image superimposed upon it. Eventually, so many past images would be trapped in the mirror that no accurate reflection of existence would be possible. When the mind rests in the eternal instant, carrying nothing from the past in the form of emotional baggage and not dreaming of a possible future, only then does the mind truly reflect the absolute universe—a reality that transcends all relative phenomena.

Chapter 5

MUGA ICHI-NEN HO MEDITATION

1. Coordinate mind and body while gently focusing the eyes on an object.

2. Do not just look but actually see.

3. Concentrate until you forget yourself and only the object remains.

4. Notice all aspects of the object, and then remove it from view.

5. You should still be able to visualize it clearly or draw it in detail.

Muga ichi-nen ho meditation is unique in that it can be practiced pretty much anywhere and at any time. Since it involves bringing the mind into the present moment, the only moment at which the body exists, muga ichi-nen ho fosters coordination of mind and body. A mental condition similar to muga ichi-nen ho is also essential in other Japanese yoga exercises. This meditation can help you become successful in Shin-shin-toitsu-do as well as transfer the insights from this Way into ordinary life.

Muga means "no self" but is maybe more easily understood as "no

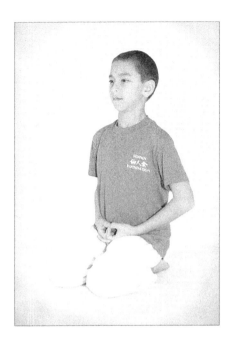

Fig. 7. Muga ichi-nen ho is often practiced using the *seiza* sitting position.

self-consciousness." *Ichi-nen* is "one thought," while *ho* is a "method" or "exercise." Be aware, however, that understanding how terms are defined isn't the same as grasping the state of mind that's being described. Real practice yields authentic, firsthand experience, which defines itself.

Muga ichi-nen ho can be practiced under most circumstances, but it's customary to use the *seiza* sitting position (Figure 7) or a full or half-lotus position (Figure 8) akin to the seated postures in Zen and Indian yoga (although it's easier to retain the proper alignment of the spine in seiza). If you're not used to sitting in such postures, try copying the illustrations precisely, but adopt these positions slowly and carefully. They're helpful for sustaining good posture and balance, but they do require flexible legs. (In Chapter 9 you'll find exercises that aid in flexibility.) You can also sit erect in a firm chair (Figure 9).

Fig. 8. Muga ichi-nen ho can also be practiced in both full and half lotus positions.

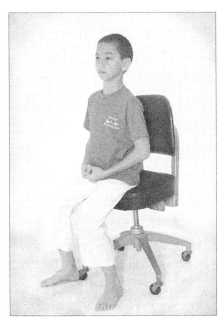

Fig. 9. You can also practice muga ichi-nen ho sitting erect in a firm chair.

Forming a circle with the thumb and index finger of each hand while interlacing the other fingers together is called an *in* in Japanese. The little finger edges of the hands should be pressed four finger widths below the navel as in the illustrations. This "in" is largely symbolic, indicating a unification of opposites, and it's comparable to the Indian *mudra*. (Being symbolic, its use in Shin-shin-toitsu-do exercises is not strictly required.) More important than the precise sitting position is the posture that you maintain while sitting. It must be an upright but relaxed position—a posture in which each body part responds to gravity and settles naturally into its appropriate place.

Discovering the Proper Posture for Meditation

During meditation, maintain a position that's relaxed and erect. Imitate the illustrations and keep in mind the following details. They're important for mind-body unification in yoga and meditation.

In seiza, sit lightly on the heels, with the big toes crossed on top of each other and some space between the knees. Even though seiza is difficult at first, for some people who are stiff it's practical for centering weight forward and down into the hara. Regard the hara as a natural center that corresponds to your center of balance and center of gravity.

Don't slump (which causes weight to slip backward and away from your hara) or lift the shoulders (which unsettles your body upward and away from your hara). Sit down lightly, as if your "bottom" were sore, and retain a relaxed carriage that looks "big."

Numerous times during meditation, and in daily life, the head sags forward. At that time, the neck collapses, curves, and shortens. This produces a "hump" at its base (near the seventh cervical vertebra). The rest of the spine before long curves in on itself as well. You can change this by concentrating on the hara and by correcting your posture with the action of your head. Mentally release your muscles, especially those along the neck and spine. Visualizing your hara as an anchor, guide the top of your head up and away from your hara. Then, draw in your chin and bring your forehead back into alignment with your lower abdomen. Allow the spine and neck to elongate until your posture is aligned. If you concentrate and relax, the body will move gradually into the correct position, with limited conscious effort. (This is similar to "willing" the fingers to touch in Experiment One in Chapter 2). However, don't coerce your body into an overly erect posture.

Attachments prevent us from being in harmony with the continual changes taking place in life. Based on this observation, is detachment the best way of dealing with matters in life and meditation?

By relaxing and applying visualization, allow your chest to expand, while the back and shoulders widen. Your ears, shoulders, and pelvis should be parallel to the ground.

Apply the same principles to half or full lotus positions. For half lotus, place the sole of your right foot against your left thigh next to the groin. Put your left foot on top of the crease formed by your bent right leg. In full lotus, place your right foot on top of your left thigh, with the heel touching the abdomen. Next, carefully lift your left foot and put it on top of your right thigh (also touching the abdomen). As always, detailed instruction must come from a qualified teacher.

In a chair, avoid sitting with legs outstretched, as this causes your pelvis to roll backward and your back to slouch. When sitting in a chair, sit with the feet flat on the floor or tucked under the chair, roughly as your legs tuck under your hips in seiza. This maintains your natural lumbar curve, and it shifts weight toward the front surface of the lower midsection—exactly where you want to center your weight and mind in the hara.

Relax your face and eyes. Find the most comfortable posture within the context of the above directions. This act of "centering" causes a particularly balanced position.

The above postural details can be practiced in everyday life for better health and less tension.

Performing Muga Ichi-nen Ho

Muga ichi-nen ho involves gazing at an object while in a condition of heightened consciousness and concentration. It's popular in India to focus attention on a candle flame, but any object will do.

Begin by aligning your posture. You should be sitting up straight, not slumping, but your carriage shouldn't be unduly rigid or erect. (Think of the feeling in your arm while doing orenai te in Chapter 3. When you did it correctly, was your arm flaccid? Was it stiff and tense? Most likely the sensation was one of suppleness without inordinate tightness or limpness—a sort of "positive relaxation." You now need to investigate how to transfer that identical feeling into your whole body so that you're "filled with ki.")

Gently focus your eyes on the candle's flame. Position it so that you can look at it in a comfortable manner and not upset your aligned posture. Allow your eyes to rest on it softly and naturally. (Some folks favor a relaxed, half-open eye position.) Avoid staring, as this will not only cause tension that hinders coordination of body and mind but also dissolve the stream of ki from the eyes that's directed toward the flame. Arm tension in orenai te is likewise unproductive.

Next, bring your attention into the present moment and allow the object of concentration to wholly fill your mind. Truly *see* the flame, as it really is, instead of just vaguely looking at it. This focuses your mind in the now (where the flame and your body exist), and it therefore helps to unite mind and body. Mental and physical harmony can only take place when we're in a natural and relaxed state. While it's vital to notice the candle flame, your concentration should not be strained but rather relaxed.

To arrive at this situation, you'll need to focus the mind intensely on the flame without attempting to "push out" other thoughts and feelings. By trying to keep out other thoughts, you actually end up thinking more about the sensations and ideas that you are trying to escape than about the object of concentration. You also set up a predicament in which you're in conflict with the sounds, smells, or feelings that you're trying to block out. This state of conflict is ultimately conflict with nature, since nature is everywhere. Philosophy aside, it's hard to relax while trying to fight off all sensory impressions that do not correspond to the flame.

Attachment and Concentration

Naturally we don't want to become attached to any particular thought or sensation since this will only distract us from what's currently right in front of us. Attachments prevent us from being in harmony with the continual changes taking place in life. Based on this observation, is detachment the best way of dealing with matters in life and meditation?

Isn't detachment a reaction—a reaction to the suffering we've experienced when we're unable to have, accomplish, or hang on to what we desire? If we observe our minds directly, we may discover that in

attempting to not be attached, we've only created another attachment—an attachment to detachment.

Muga equals the transcendence of the artificial self, the self that
believes in itself as a genuine entity, separate from the rest of the universe. This self, being the product of memories, past thoughts, and the
impressions others have had about it, has no firm reality and, being
separate from the universe, will not survive death. To deal with this fear
of nonbeing, it attaches itself to possessions, people, beliefs, definite
conclusions, and even thoughts. But all of this is impermanent as well,
and the illusory self continues in its attachment, creating a vicious circle of suffering.

The separate, artificial self attaches itself to conclusions, thoughts,
and things in an attempt for permanency and then seeks detachment
when this painfully fails. Both attachment and detachment are protec-
tive reflexes of a self that has no permanent reality.

Muga and Concentration

Rather than aiming for a forced concentration, think of letting
your attention rest on the candle's light in an uncontrived fashion. Pay
attention to every element of the flame until you forget yourself and
just the flame remains. This is the state of muga ichi-nen. Self-consciousness drops away until your flame becomes the "one thought." In
muga ichi-nen, no walls exist between you and nature. The mind is
peaceful, resting in tune with the universe, and time ceases.

Many of us have experienced engaging in some act that we delight
in so profoundly that we forget ourselves and suspend our sense of
time. When we consolidate the mind and body in the moment, con-

centrating deeply without self-consciousness, just the action taking place fills our senses.

Plainly stated, when we're cheerful and at peace, we seldom dwell on ourselves. Even on a completely physical level, we rarely spend the day conscious of our thumb unless it hurts. When our thumb feels fine, we don't pay a great deal of attention to it. (This, naturally, does not mean that we cannot or should not be able to become aware of different parts of ourselves.)

In fact, self-image leads to suffering. Consider the emotion of anger. When we're angry, where does the anger come from? We're in pain, and we react against the pain. Perhaps another person has said something about us that we feel is insult-

ing, untrue, or unkind. Why would this cause us pain, and thus anger? Is it because our self-image has been attacked? If so, then the image we have of our-

Many of us live in a world of ideas, ideals, symbols, and memories. Muga ichi-nen ho gives us a chance to enter the realm of actuality, to focus the mind on what is.

selves must relate to our experience of anger. No self-image, no anger. And is it also true that if there is no self-image, there is no jealousy, no fear, or other problems in life? There's only one way to find out.

Why do we create and work ceaselessly to sustain an image of our-selves at all? An image that's usually based on our past experiences—what we *were* as opposed to what we *are*—and the opinions other people have about us. If we face the reality of what we actually are at this moment, is a self-image needed? We create an image or symbolic representation of something when either the real entity is not present or we don't genuinely know the real thing. Because we don't know our genuine nature and that of the universe (which aren't necessarily separate), we react with anger or fear whenever we think the image that we've created is being attacked—an image that is all we know and that serves to distract us from the reality of our true existence.

If I see the truth about myself, no one can upset me deeply. If I'm pretending to be a peaceful person or striving toward a self-created ideal of peacefulness, I'll become angry when I'm told that I have a bad temper. Yet if I actually am an angry person, to be told that is to simply see what is a fact. Until this fact is really seen for what it is, no change is possible.

Then, who changes? Do we know ourselves, or merely our self-created image? Is this image necessary, and does our genuine self emerge if we drop the image to encounter existence just as it is? Does the self exist as a separate, distinct entity? What exactly does the "no self" in muga ichi-nen refer to?

Many of us live in a world of ideas, ideals, symbols, and memories. Muga ichi-nen ho gives us a chance to enter the realm of actuality, to focus the mind on *what is*.

As you focus on the flickering flame, try to detect the line that separates the person that sees the light and the light itself. Does this line of demarcation exist as a set reality or an artificial fabrication? (To paraphrase Indian spiritual teacher Jiddhu Krishnamurti, "Can you separate the observer from the observed?") Test this meditation instead of trying to guess a solution. It's an important inquiry. In an absolute sense, does a solid line exist that separates humanity from nature and one human being from another? Muga ichi-nen ho aims at an undivided union of mind, body, and the universe. Traditionally, each of the Japanese Do forms has had an equivalent mission.

The Object vs. Knowledge of the Object

When we look at the object of concentration in this meditation, are we seeing the actual object or merely our knowledge of the object? Perhaps you've never considered this question before, but there is a difference.

Actual awareness, taking place in the moment, is fundamentally different from our knowledge of something, which is rooted in the past. Suppose you're using a computer as your object of concentration. Seeing with awareness means seeing the actual fact of the computer that's sitting in front of you. Once we say to ourselves, "This computer has a certain kind of hard drive" or "This computer cost way too much money, and pretty soon I'm going to have to replace it for yet another newer and better version," we're observing our opinions and knowledge of the object of concentration but not the genuine object.

When we experience meditation, we leap into the undiscovered moment, into the ever-changing now, completely stripped of assumption, opinion, and anything clinging to yesterday.

The object of concentration is, in some ways, not the point. In this meditation, we're working on seeing with total awareness, which doesn't inevitably even require an object to focus upon. We're not so much trying to see this thing or hear that other thing, but rather trying to enter into a state of pure, uncorrupted awareness of the universe at this instant.

All of this is, of course, not to say that we should not retain background information about a variety of things in life. However, this information should be something we can use as a tool when and where we want to use it. It shouldn't take over and dominate the mind, preventing us from truly seeing and learning that which is new. And when the mind is in the moment, everything is fresh, new, and alive. The mind never grows old or jaded.

Testing the Muga Ichi-nen State of Being

Try closing your eyes at some time in your meditation. Can you nevertheless recall the details of the flame? (It is an even more interesting test of attention if you use a more detailed object as your focus.) We're so used to just glancing at the environment through the eyes of the past that we're frequently not certain if we are in fact paying attention or if we merely *think* that we're paying attention. Dynamic meditation in everyday existence involves the act of truthfully *seeing*.

Many of us have changed some aspect of our appearance only to have this go unnoticed by friends. Perhaps you've shaved off a mustache, added a tattoo, or altered your hairstyle, but your acquaintances failed to initially notice. In such a case, your friends were looking at their environment through the eyes of the past instead of actually *seeing* what was taking place in the present.

Closing your eyes is one method of testing yourself. Even having a friend ask you questions about the details of the object once it's removed from view can be used as a test of attention and, thus, mind and body coordination. The mind must truly perceive what the body is looking at.

You can also try turning away from the object of concentration after some time has gone by and attempt to draw it. (A candle flame is possibly not the best subject matter. Something with more concrete details can be drawn more easily.) Don't worry about artistic ability; the principal goal is to see if you have absorbed the details of what you've been looking at. (This is another method of testing your power of attention, and it's a fun technique to help children cultivate greater concentration.)

Muga ichi-nen ho is an ideal means of cultivating artistic aptitude. Drawing and nearly all other forms of art are, in fact, exercises in precise observation. For instance, it's not unusual for art students sketching a still life to place shadows on the wrong side of objects. This is not a matter of poor technique or understanding so much as an inability to clearly notice the world. This act of "noticing" is a pivotal element in all arts, including Shin-shin-toitsu-do, and it's related to meditation. In a very real way, it *is* meditation.

Muga ichi-nen ho is such a simple technique that its essence is largely summed up in the five points at the start of this chapter. However, while the technique really only consists of those five elements, what allows us to enter into the state of muga ichi-nen, what keeps us from realizing that state, and what happens when we're in the muga ichi-nen condition are subjects that contain a vast number of profound dimensions. Examining these dimensions is as important as the simple technique of muga ichi-nen ho.

Dropping the Object of Concentration

When we begin muga ichi-nen ho, we're studying the nature of the mind and concentration by focusing attention on a single subject. This is concentration with an object, but in concentrating on whatever it is, we tend to become attached to it and to use it for motivation. As long as concentration is linked to a specific thing, requiring ongoing and deliberate conscious effort, concentration cannot be sustained naturally in everyday life. Coordination of mind, body, and the universe takes place continuously and freely only when attention is maintained naturally, without necessarily having a particular object of concentration and without conscious effort or motive.

Now, without taking your eyes off of the candle flame, discover how to maintain this heightened state of awareness without any dependence on the flame itself. In other words, your attention takes in everything without limiting itself to the candle. This is concentration without an object. Once it's discovered, you should be able to walk away from what you were gazing at and fully attend to each object that comes before your eyes or is in some way perceived by any of your senses. In short, you display full concentration in relationship to each moment and each experience in life, no matter how quickly they follow each other. Each moment is lived fully, and when the next moment comes, it too is completely experienced without any shadow of the prior moment diluting your full concentration.

Isn't detachment a reaction—a reaction to the suffering we've experienced when we're unable to have, accomplish, or hang on to what we desire? If we observe our minds directly, we may discover that in attempting to not be attached, we've only created another attachment—an attachment to detachment.

To shift from concentration with an object to concentration without an object is vital. Still, explaining how to accomplish this shift, and even more importantly how to sustain it, is arduous at best. Each of us needs to discover this through experimentation, and muga ichi-nen ho gives us a framework within which to experiment.

Here are a few hints and observations. Try thinking of shifting from concentration with a motive to concentration without a motive. Sustain the feeling of attention while dropping the consciousness of focusing on a particular thing for a specific reason. Try shifting from concentration that's exclusive to concentration that excludes nothing.

Discover objectless concentration through a process of negation. For example, while you continue to look at the given object, notice if anything is causing or motivating your concentration. Intensity of mind with a cause isn't objectless attention. Do you sense any attachment to your ability to concentrate or to the subject of your concentration? That's not it either. Feeling absorbed in something? What you're absorbed in is the object of concentration, so that can't be it. A feeling of exclusion? That's exclusion from everything that isn't the object of concentration. A struggle, a sense of division, a search for a result—all of these relate to concentration with an object. Discover what object-less concentration *is not* to uncover what *it is*.

When concentration has a goal, we frequently experience attachment to that goal, and attachment leads to suffering. Is it possible to guide the mind with great intensity in a certain direction, with no ending goal in sight, without stopping attention and ki at any specific point? Is it possible to focus the mind fully without attachment? Let's find out, because for many of us attention only comes when we cling to something—a person, a belief, . . . a candle flame. And when that object of attachment is lost or extinguished (for nothing is permanent), we find ourselves empty and uncentered. Yet concentration without an object is not something to cling to either, because this is just replacing one attachment with another. And the cycle starts all over again. What takes place when we face this fact in meditation?

In the next chapter, we'll examine *anjo daza ho,* in which we focus on the sound of a bell instead of an object. You concentrate completely on the tone just as you've concentrated on the candle flame. However, unlike the candle, the resonance of the bell fades, so you'll experiment with letting the object of concentration fall away while the sensation of concentrating continues without a specific object of concentration. Anjo daza ho is easier in the sense that it gives us a clear-cut approach to moving toward objectless concentration. But it is harder because we don't get to decide when we're ready to make such a shift. Like everything in life, once the sound is born, it's already disappearing.

After practicing anjo daza ho, come back to muga ichi-nen ho. Try approaching it from the perspective of what you've been experimenting with in the other form of meditation. Ultimately, these two forms are the same. They merely make use of different senses to lead to the same objectless attention as well as mind-body coordination.

About the Word "Meditation"

Meditation as a word can mean many different things to many different people. In fact, its meaning varies so greatly from person to person as to make communication difficult. Be careful about assuming that your definition of meditation is the same one that's being used in this book. (This advice holds true for all definitions and communication between people in general.)

Knowledge, which relates to the repository of memory, only becomes problematic when it's no longer a tool and overrides our instant-to-instant understanding of what's really taking place. If you had never heard of meditation or read any books about it, how would you begin? (You'll find this question repeated in varying forms throughout this work. It is a vital inquiry that lies at the very heart of meditation itself.)

To grab onto the words or experiences of others regarding meditation, especially when words and methods vary so greatly, and to attempt to match your actions against such words isn't personal understanding of meditation. It's copying. And while copying in life is useful for learning certain techniques, exercises, or methods, meditation is not a "thing" to be copied. It is an experience. An experience that cannot be forced, imitated, given, or borrowed from another—an instantaneous experience that's not based on prior knowledge or rooted in the past.

Coordination of mind, body, and the universe takes place continuously and freely only when attention is maintained naturally, without necessarily having a particular object of concentration and without conscious effort or motive.

When we experience meditation, we leap into the undiscovered moment, into the ever-changing now, completely stripped of assumption, opinion, and anything clinging to yesterday. It is to experience existence without projecting our past onto reality, to discover and encounter life fully. Meditation isn't a projection of hopes, aspirations, mental creations, or our "selves." It is not created, least of all by us. And it is beyond time.

Entering into the Timeless

Our beliefs, biases, and opinions stem from past experiences that we've recorded as memory. Memory only becomes problematic when it becomes conditioning. Eventually, many of us feel that we're "stuck in a rut," having the same problems in varying permutations over and over again. Jiko anji (discussed in Chapter 3) offers an immediate way of altering particularly destructive kinds of conditioning, and although this is useful, we must still wonder if it's possible to have functional memory yet not be conditioned by our past.

This isn't to say that certain conditioned reflexes are inevitably problematic. Hitting your car horn when another automobile turns in front of you is a useful reflex. The conditioning of techniques, methods, and physical reflexes is not the issue, but psychological and emotional conditioning is. Is it possible to experience life fully and yet not be conditioned psychologically by the experience (to remain free from "emotional baggage")? Muga ichi-nen ho and related forms of meditation represent opportunities to discover the nature of ourselves for ourselves. And what we discover will by definition be unknown, or it's not a discovery at all. Still, by clinging to past knowledge and experiences, we often end up discovering only what we want to find or what we've previously experienced in a modified form.

We long for security, and we hope to find it by maintaining set beliefs or by accumulating possessions—a college degree, a favorite car, the perfect house—even our spouses can be a "thing" to be possessed. Does any of this work? Our parents, our society, and yes, even ourselves have conditioned us to believe that somehow all of this will give us the security of "the good life." But beliefs can be challenged, and when they're severely attacked, we go to war to defend them. War is the least secure state imaginable.

What of the house, which can burn down; the car, which can be stolen; the college degree, which lands us a job from which we can be laid off? When we encounter such problems we simultaneously encounter fear because we're forced to look at how much of an illusion security actually is. Seeing this, we are transformed . . . right? Nope. We recoil from that which challenges our conditioning, and buy an even more high-tech alarm for our next car to ensure "true security."

Only a mind that recognizes continuity but doesn't seek or anticipate continuity can accurately perceive the instant . . . the instant that is not inevitably a perpetuation of past patterns and that is ageless. Such a mind is in timeless meditation.

Security is sought by memory, which seeks to continue the known or the past. A mind that is attached to the past is conditioned. Our past moves into the present, then the future, by means of the conditioned mind, and it is this mind that longs for security, even when it's seen to be an illusion, so that it may perpetuate itself. Each of us who has identified this conditioned mind as our actual self feels that to lose this conditioning, this continuation of past experience, is to lose our very self—to cease to exist.

Some of us then realize that we're trapped by the past, which has conditioned our present and our future. We seek to leap out of time, to find freedom in continuous change. Being in fear and trapped by our very notion of ourselves, we long for the timeless. Yet even such an action toward a state beyond time is coming from our knowledge of what's happened to us in the past. It's a seeking that's still based on try-ing to find a condition beyond fear—a condition of security. It is grasp-ing at another form of security, and this grasping based on fear cannot lead us beyond fear. Thus it fails as a step into the unknown, an action that's not of time and memory.

What then is meditation that is outside of time? It cannot be forced or created. Any deliberate attempt at creation stems from what we think meditation should be, which is in turn based on what we've previously heard or thought about meditation. It's not meditation itself. It is of the past.

To attempt to preserve continuity is to be caught in time. Reality is now. Real life is now as well, and the same can be said of meditation. In the now, we can discover reality and whether continuity is taking place at all. It's the assumption of permanence that prevents the mind from seeing what really is taking place in a state beyond time.

When I was younger, I participated in judo competitions on local, regional, and national levels. Like most sports, judo has certain strate-gies. One simple strategy is to take note of patterns detected in an opponent's attacks and movements. Suppose the opponent tries to sweep your lead leg out from under you. As he attempts this sweep, you step back to dodge it. He then attacks with a hip throw, which you block.

A few seconds later, the same thing happens again. You've detected a pattern, and so you deliberately leave your leg extended, inviting the sweep, hoping for the subsequent hip throw that you'll then counter to win the match. Sounds good, right?

Once I felt my opponent was starting to anticipate a certain series of movements from me, I would deliberately and carefully recreate what he was looking for to give him a sense of continuity. Then, when he thought he knew what would come after my foot sweep, I would suddenly break my self-created pattern, unbalancing him and sometimes winning.

Here's the point: I consciously created a pattern that gave him a feeling of continuity, but this continuity was a lie. Only a mind that recognizes continuity but doesn't seek or anticipate continuity can accurately perceive the instant . . . the instant that is not inevitably a perpetuation of past patterns and that is ageless. Such a mind is in timeless meditation.

ZEN: *"innate goodness," painted in the semicursive style of the famed calligrapher Ogishi. Nakamura Tempu taught that people are born in an essentially pure state but sometimes accumulate harmful habits. While habits may be bad, humanity is inherently good. Meditation is seeing into our innate nature and that of the universe. Its goal is to discover an intrinsic virtue, compassion, and connection with all creations that is not the result of social pressure, conditioning, copying, or wishful thinking.*

Chapter 6

ANJO DAZA HO MEDITATION

1. Sit with mind and body unified.

2. Focus on the sound of the bell.

3. Mentally follow the decreasing waves to achieve muga ichi-nen.

4. As the waves become infinitely small, continue listening.

5. Let your listening expand, so that your ki extends into infinite space.

Many features of muga ichi-nen ho, such as proper posture, relaxed concentration in the present, lack of self-consciousness, and the outward motion of ki, are also found in anjo daza ho meditation. You can use the same seiza, lotus, or seated positions for this method as well. The benefits of muga ichi-nen ho are likewise associated with anjo daza ho.

Anjo characterizes a "peaceful feeling." *Daza* concerns striking a meditation bell while in a seated position, and *ho* is a "method" or "exercise." The metal, bowl-shaped Japanese bell used here is called a

143

rin. Hitting the edge of the bell with its accompanying wooden striker creates a mellow gong-type tone. This bell, which is at times associated with Buddhist rituals, can sustain a lengthy resonance (depending on its size and the quality of the metal used) and has a calming effect. (To learn where to buy a rin, see the back of this book.)

Engaging in Anjo Daza Ho

You begin anjo daza ho by adopting a seated pose in which you can maintain a proper posture as well as the union of mind and body. Lightly close your eyes. Avoid shutting them firmly or abruptly because this will produce meditation-inhibiting tension.

Hit the bell cleanly one time and focus your attention on the tone produced (Figure 10). Once more, this is "relaxed concentration." Attempting to block out other sounds and thoughts only diverts you from the resonance of the bell that you're mentally following. Let the bell's note fill your whole mind to become the "one thought." When your mind contains this single thought completely, while not trying to drive other sensory impressions out, your self is forgotten. Muga ichi-nen is attained, and no division exists between you and the universe (in which the sound resonates).

Nonetheless, unlike the candle's flame in muga ichi-nen ho, the bell's tone is gradually fading, growing dimmer like the image of ki traveling away from you in orenai te. If meditating on the reverberation leads to ichi-nen, or "one thought," then as the mind follows the declining tone, it progressively arrives at *mu-nen,* "no thoughts." To use a popular Japanese analogy, mu-nen is a mental condition that's totally still, like a pond with no waves.

Fig. 10. Anjo daza ho uses a seated pose. The eyes are closed lightly. Strike the bell cleanly once and focus on the tone produced so that it becomes "one thought."

Once this individual note fills your mind to form one thought, pursue the decreasing waves of sound. If real concentration has been achieved, your brain waves grow gradually smaller as do the sound waves. In plain English, although all living brains show brain-wave patterns, it's possible to arrive at a continually smaller and calmer pattern of waves. The bell's sound merely leads us in this direction. Think of it as a resonance that's infinitely decreasing.

As the sound waves grow infinitely smaller, keep pursuing them mentally. Even when you can no longer perceive the sound, let the feeling and state of mind that's been produced continue on its own. The secret is to "do nothing," and then the condition of tranquility will not be changed.

On the Path to the Infinite

Since these ideas are in reality universal, the same approach for calming the mind can be utilized by making use of bodily movement or visualized images. For instance, brush motion in Japanese calligraphy can even become a medium for meditation.

Assume you're grasping a brush above your paper. Leaving your elbow down and in a relaxed condition, move the brush repeatedly from left to right in an arc of around 12 inches. As you do this, focus your mind resolutely on the action of the brush tip. Next, progressively make the size of the arc smaller and smaller.

Shodo (Japanese calligraphy) students notice that if they keep their mind centered on the brush tip, their brain-wave patterns also grow smaller and calmer. In a short while, the motion becomes so small that it's not outwardly noticeable. The mental representation of ever-reducing movement falls away, but an experienced practitioner will let the feeling of tranquility continue infinitely. If you're having difficulty conceiving what this looks like, tie a rock or relatively heavy object to a string. Start it swinging sideways, then hold your hand motionless. The object's arc will become successively smaller until it seems to be hanging still. You can do something comparable with a brush, except allow the sensation of endless reduction to go on within you.

Once Japanese calligraphy students get the hang of it, the above procedure can help them to still the movement of their brush even when their projection of ki through the brush hasn't achieved this. This "infinite reduction approach" is more than a potent method of stilling the brush and mind. We'll use a related reduction technique later in this book when we explore *yodo ho* exercises. Since we cannot envision infinity intellectually, this method has the ultimate capacity to lead us to a state of transcendence that is both immeasurable and everlasting.

In shodo, students can use their brush as an object of mental focus to guide the mind toward tranquility. You can use the endlessly decreasing bell tone to achieve the identical purpose. In fact, whether you use a decreasing tone, a decreasing physical movement, or simply the mental representation of infinite reduction, it's possible to arrive at a similar state. The principle of endless reduction leading to a condition of doing nothing is

When we stick a name on something, we cease to fully perceive its genuine, present nature, perceiving instead everything we already know and believe about the word rather than experiencing completely what's before our eyes or ears right now.

what is significant, not the device that leads to it—a device that should be abandoned when no longer necessary.

As part of "doing nothing," continue to listen even when the bell's note is no longer loud enough to be perceived. Unless this state of sustained listening and attention is held after the sound has faded, calmness will fade as well. When we can no longer perceive the bell, what are we listening to? In a sense, you're listening to the universe. At this time, allow your listening to expand to fill the universe so that the universe itself becomes the "one thought." It is this union with the universe that is embodied by the term *toitsu*, or "unification."

And what if you lose concentration at some point? Just hit the bell and begin again. (Novices might do well to purchase a top-quality large bell, which sustains tone longer.) Second, how long you practice anjo daza ho, as with muga ichi-nen ho, is up to you. Many people begin with 15 minutes as a standard. Employing these forms of meditation before practicing other aspects of Japanese yoga is ideal for calming the mind and harmonizing with nature. Plus, since this meditation consists of listening to what's taking place in the instant, it brings the mind into the present, where the body resides, producing unification of mind and body.

As far as technique goes, that's about all there is to anjo daza ho. Like muga ichi-nen ho, the method is simple. But what takes place while engaging in this technique and what it means in terms of meditation and daily living is quite profound. As we practice anjo daza ho, it's important to consider the nature of listening, concentration, and time.

Concentration without Attachment

The qualities cultivated to arrive at muga ichi-nen are as meaningful as the condition that's cultivated. Although these qualities are multifaceted, one main point is the capability to concentrate the mind without having it "get stuck" anywhere or at any time. To illustrate, if we focus ki on a flame or an audible resonance, we cannot arrive at muga ichi-nen without discovering how to deal with external stimuli and our thoughts, all of which can divert the mind from the object of concentration. If your mind "gets stuck" on an outer sound or an internal sound (a thought), it's no longer centered on the bell's resonance. If you try to block out these noises, your mind's still fighting them, and you've set up a conflict-ridden condition.

However, suppose that you are sitting in front of a busy street. Across the street you see something that grabs your attention. As you observe the spectacle, people are passing through your line of sight. Do you turn your head to track each person, or do you just notice the passing individuals while keeping your attention focused on what you're viewing?

The bell's pitch or the flame is what you're watching, while exterior stimuli and internal thoughts are the passing people. Note all thoughts and feelings without mentally commenting on them or letting the mind attach itself to them. Just silently "watch" the note of the bell, and "do nothing."

Just as there's usually a space or interval between people passing on the street, even if it sometimes seems very small, a space also exists between thoughts. In your meditation, see if you can perceive this

Whatever thoughts or internal conflicts come up—do nothing. Do not try to force them to cease or change. . . . Genuine attention has no motive.

gap between thoughts. What is it, and does it belong to the realm of time? If it does not, then it's unborn and undying, beyond all conditioning, which is a psychological carry-over from the past to the present.

Whatever thoughts or internal conflicts come up—*do nothing*. Do not try to force them to cease or change. And don't "do nothing" to still the mind, quiet fears, or resolve conflicts—all of this is *doing something*. It only leads to more struggling and prevents you from seeing the actual nature of thought and internal conflict. Genuine attention has no motive.

This observation or listening doesn't involve effort. Effort merely distracts you from what's taking place in the instant. A kind of concentration exists that's not forced. We've all experienced listening or paying attention to something we truly enjoyed. At that moment, was effort required for concentration to take place?

Wordless Concentration

Similarly, there is no necessity to attach a word or label to each thought or sensation. Anjo daza ho requires a relaxed concentration that perceives the essence of life beyond words. While words are needed for communication, they have limitations. Frequently, when we stick a name on something, we cease to fully perceive its genuine, present nature, perceiving instead everything we already know and believe about *the word* rather than experiencing completely what's before our eyes or ears right now.

In a very real sense, we're translating reality rather than seeing it as it is. That's why when two or more people view an event, frequently two or more interpretations of what took place result. Each individual translates reality based on his or her prejudices, fears, and conditioning as opposed to the facts. Is it then possible for us to see existence as it is—to see the actual nature of reality before interpretation takes place?

This question is of tremendous importance. We live in an age in which we're experiencing war, starvation, and racial violence. These are facts. However, each person, organization, and nation "translates" and interprets these facts based on prior experiences, attachments, fears, and desires. So while the fact of widespread famine in some areas is indisputable, each country and representative often fails to see the simple facts of the problem. With each camp having a different translation of reality, conflict is inevitable. This is extremely problematic as it implies that multiple versions of reality exist. Is this actually the case? Or does the fact of war or starvation, simple and clear, only become complex when different individuals begin to translate present reality based on their biases and particular prior conditioning? Perhaps it's only when humanity evolves to see life for what

Some people are mature and responsible at sixteen, while certain sixty-year-olds shouldn't be left alone with sharp objects. Rather than seeing who we genuinely are, or viewing a person's ability and maturity by their actions, we see them and ourselves through the veil of age.

it is, rather than what each individual thinks it is or should be, that humanity will arrive at harmony. In anjo daza ho, we face a reality that exists beyond words, translations, and interpretations.

The bottom line is this: since our ability to place a word with a given perception stems from our past knowledge and experiences, the act of labeling during meditation can keep the mind from arriving at a direct, unaltered observation of the present. Do nothing, and in a sense, "say nothing" during meditation. Concentration without attachment is vital for all types of meditation. In a manner of speaking, it is meditation itself.

Ultimately, even the object of concentration must drop away (in this example, the bell's sound) until only uncorrupted attention without attachment remains and rests in the eternity of the moment. It's a moment outside of the shackles of time that is free of attachment and its associated suffering and has no divisions within and no barriers without. This is Shin-shin-toitsu-do—"the Way of mind and body unification"—but it is likewise the fundamental heart of all of the Ways.

Releasing Past Influences and Moving Beyond Time

In anjo daza ho, we reach a point where the object of concentration fades but full attention remains—objectless concentration. But we have a strong tendency to become attached to past experiences, which is why we find it difficult to allow the bell's tone to fade, and then do nothing. Even the present becomes something to cling to, reducing the present to the past. (The instant we say, "This is the present," that moment has already become the past.)

Let's examine this together with the idea of using the following comments as a catalyst for observing our minds even more seriously but not as a doctrine to be memorized or believed.

In the previous chapter, we looked at how the mind seeks security as a way of sustaining an image of the self. The real self exists. It has no need of a representation of itself. We create such a representation to deal with the fact that we have no firm knowledge of the self and its relationship to the universe. To perpetuate this artificial self, we seek an illusory security in many forms—our attachment to pleasure and pain is but one example.

In the past, we underwent something painful. We then sometimes go to great lengths to avoid all future pain, and this avoidance is fear stemming from the past. It's important to realize several points in regard to pain (if only because some of the exercises in the book can be painful at first).

Pain is a reaction. It happens. It's not a reaction that is fully within our control, and it has an informative purpose. We strive to avoid it because of a desire to preserve things the way they are, even when we realize that pain is an automatic reaction that is completely impossible to avoid. We work to preserve the status quo, which is sought by a mind that's clinging to the past and caught in time.

Pain, like pleasure, is a transitory and inevitable part of living. Suffering, however, is optional.

Pain and injury are not inevitably the same. Pain is frequently momentary, while injury can be permanent. Something can be painful but not injurious and even good for you. (Stretching is an excellent example.) To avoid injury, on the other hand, is common sense. To live in fear of pain is to live in a world of past pain.

Pain and suffering are also not the same. We cannot completely avoid pain and couldn't function safely in life without the ability to feel pain. Pain, like pleasure, is a transitory and inevitable part of living. Suffering, however, is optional. We create it by holding onto past experiences, attaching ourselves to the previous experience of pain, and living in fear of it. This refusal to release the past creates an attachment that breeds fear and becomes an origin of suffering. It is, moreover, a form of suffering itself.

Fear is of the past. We're afraid of different matters rooted in past associations and experiences. What's more, even when we are afraid of the possibility of a future occurrence, we're using previous experiences to extrapolate about the future. Fear is of the past, but action exists in the present. Anjo daza ho is also in the present, and all effective action must function there as well.

We've heard of being frozen with fear. This also relates to a mind that's frozen in the past moment. When the mind is in the present, it merely acts. As the present is beyond time, there's no time to be afraid, only to do. The mind perceives, the body acts—mind and body coordination.

Likewise, our desire to hold onto pleasure gives birth to fear and suffering. The wish to sustain pleasure, recreate pleasure, or find pleasure is a desire stemming from our past. We feel great pleasure during a given event. It may be emotional enjoyment, sexual pleasure, or pleasure in some other form, yet rarely do we plan such events. Like pain, pleasure is a reaction—a reaction we cannot fully control.

Can we plan to experience pleasure? Certainly we may lay out a fun outing and, in the process of going to dinner and a movie, feel moments of pleasure. But is this guaranteed? Can we say that since we're eating a fine dinner, we will now feel pleasure? Probably not. There are too many variables.

Along the same lines, once we experience pleasure, can we recreate it? We certainly try, but this is just the mind's attachment to carrying the past into the present in a vain attempt to create pleasure at some time in the future.

Even when we manage to recreate similar events, the pleasure we sense is never the same. Moreover, by measuring pleasure we perceive against past pleasure, we destroy any chance of a deeply pleasurable experience in the present. Some people say that such-and-such is never as good as they remember it, which is undoubtedly true. The initial experience of pleasure wasn't planned, it occurred spontaneously in the moment and was fully felt by a mind that was not comparing. When comparison based on the past enters the equation, the ability to completely live through the present moment, with the full intensity of the mind, is lost. Any sensation of pleasure is dulled.

Like all sensation and all reactions, pleasure cannot be sustained. It comes and goes of its own accord. Still, we try to retain this sensation, which is impossible. And striving to accomplish the impossible leads to suffering and fear. We suffer from basically banging our heads against a wall, from trying to preserve that which can't be preserved. We're afraid that we may not be able to retain the sensation of pleasure because we equate pleasure with happiness. Is the occurrence of pleasure happiness? Is the avoidance of pain happiness?

It's possible to feel pleasure repeatedly through the repetitive use of drugs, sex, fine food, and other potentially pleasurable activities. Certainly we wouldn't use drugs if they didn't feel good. Yet the dosage tends to continue to rise since "it doesn't seem as good as before." Are people addicted to drugs or anything else happy people? Especially when they're caught in the never-ending and useless attempt to find, sustain, and recreate pleasure. As a society, we recognize the futility of drug addiction. We don't recognize, however, that even if we are not drug addicts, we still possess the root of addiction. It is the mind's addiction and attachment to past sensation.

Is the avoidance of pain happiness? It's possible to go without feeling pain for some time, but are we always happy during this time period? Again, probably not.

I'll make no attempt to define happiness, but I will ask us to mutually consider whether pleasure or the absence of pain equals real happiness. And if pleasure and pain are momentary reactions, which are ultimately beyond our control, then is it possible to discover a happiness that is not a reaction?

A reaction implies cause and effect, which in turn relates to time. Moving from cause to effect is moving from the past to the future. All of this is fixed in the mind's artificial creation of time. Time, at least on some levels, is definitely contrived by humanity. Life is not time. We end up being used by a self-created tool instead of making use of it when needed, mistaking this artificial creation for reality itself. Reality is right now. Now is beyond time.

A mind in meditation isn't trapped by the accumulation of time. It fully perceives each moment, then lets that moment die so that a genuinely fresh and vibrant new moment can be born.

Our conditioning, fears, and suffering are all rooted in the past, in time. In anjo daza ho, doing nothing means to carry nothing over from the past to arrive at a pure, unmodified perception of a moment beyond time. It means to let go of all past psychological attachments and undergo a continual rebirth from moment to moment.

It is in the instant that the mind moves beyond time and beyond age. A mind in the moment is ageless.

We often long for youth even when we realize that numerous aspects of childhood were sometimes less than pleasant. We may state that we'd like a younger, healthier body, but even those that are healthy and in their twenties often crave for a return to the past. Are we yearning for a return to adolescence, or are we actually looking back at a period in which everything was fresh and vibrant?

When the mind holds onto each past emotion and experience, the past itself becomes a weight we must carry into the present and the future. Each time we latch onto a particular fear or painful occurrence, instead of living these experiences fully and then letting them fall away, we create and maintain what amounts to an open wound. Eventually, the mind accumulates so many such "wounds" that it becomes scarred. And just as real scar tissue is relatively insensitive, our minds become jaded and dulled to all but the most extreme sensations. This is why some of us, over time, seek more and more extreme forms of sensation just to feel something. Like other forms of addiction, this attachment to sensation keeps escalating.

For instance, as children even a simple trip to the grocery store could be a moment of joy and excitement, or finding an unusual rock might be a wondrous event. But as adults whose minds have accumulated too much, not even a vacation to the jungles of the Amazon is enough.

Because our minds have built up so many layers of yesterday, we're unable to feel or perceive life without interpreting and translating it into the language of the past. Nothing's new, and we find ourselves with an old mind that's gradually worn down and weighed down by clinging to former experiences.

Our close identification with chronological age furthers this wearing down of the mind. Age, in terms of a number of years, is as artificial as time. Some people are mature and responsible at sixteen, while certain sixty-year-olds shouldn't be left alone with sharp objects. Rather than seeing who we genuinely are, or viewing a person's ability and maturity by their actions, we see them and ourselves through the veil of age. We see the idea or the representation but not the reality of life itself.

Life is constant and ever-changing. It cannot really be reduced to hours on a clock face, months on a calendar, or candles on a birthday cake. In some cultures, babies are thought to be one year old when they're born. So how old are we really? What month or year is it actually? Obviously the sequential measuring of age and time has a practical function, but in forgetting the artificial, self-created nature of all of this, we engender a mind that focuses on the image rather than the fact, a mind that's caught in time. In anjo daza ho, we transcend time.

A mind in meditation isn't trapped by the accumulation of time. It fully perceives each moment, then lets that moment die so that a genuinely fresh and vibrant new moment can be born. We perceive beyond time and age when we listen without effort or motive and see without clinging to what's seen. This instant cannot be measured and lasts forever without growing old. That instant is now.

Listening in the Moment

Just as muga ichi-nen ho involves the sense of sight, anjo daza ho makes use of our hearing capacity. Listening is an essential aspect of this exercise, but what does it mean to truly listen?

We've heard people say that a certain person "only hears what he wants to hear." Most of us have some idea what that expression means, but to what degree does this phrase also relate to us, and perhaps most of humanity?

Let's try another common phrase: "He may be listening, but he's got his own agenda." When we listen, how many of us *don't* have our own agenda? And if this is the case, do we perceive what is really being said, or do we actually perceive only our own thoughts about what's being stated? Our thoughts stem from past experiences and carry with them our desires, prejudices, and conditioning. When we listen through this veil of attachments and personal biases, are we genuinely listening to what's being said in the moment, or are we only hearing ourselves? If we're listening to ourselves, carrying past "emotional baggage" with us, perhaps this is why many of us feel like we're caught in a loop, incapable of transformation.

In communicating with others, we're commonly communicating with our image of them as much as we are talking or listening to the real person. For example, we may have had certain experiences in the past with a friend, and we've formed a certain impression of this person based on these prior experiences. It may or may not be an accurate impression, and it definitely consists of static, past ideas about our friend, who is a living, changing being. So, are we listening and talking to the person current-ly in front of us, or are we listening and reacting to *our impression* of this individual? And what if our acquaintance also perceives only his mental picture of us,

The Way of the universe can be encountered in every aspect of existence—from the most ordinary to the most extraordinary.

based on his previous experiences with us as well as his own desires and fears? Instead of two human beings in communion, we have two artificial images from the past bouncing off each other. Maybe this is why so many people feel that genuine communication is difficult.

We may say that we love our spouse, our parents, or even the world as a whole. But this statement of love implies relationship. Is any true relationship possible, if our connection with the world or with another is based as much on former impressions, personal images, and self-created ideas as it is on present facts or reality? Can mental images, which are based on past memories and have no bona fide present reality, experience love? An image or memory is never as real as the world that's passing before our eyes and ears.

Muga ichi-nen ho and anjo daza ho involve an act of direct observation and attention. It is a state that can be sustained in all our relationships, both personal and impersonal. When the film of the past is dissolved from our eyes and ears, when we genuinely perceive the person that stands in front of us, only then is a real connection made. It's a connection in which the artificial self of past memories and conditioning falls away . . . and what remains is love. Not love as pleasure, desire, attachment, or a balm for the lonely, which are common, fleeting sorts of "love," but something altogether different.

Practicing Japanese Yoga Exercises

No specific art is necessary for discovering the spirit of the Way. The Way of the universe can be encountered in every aspect of existence—from the most ordinary to the most extraordinary. Shin-shin-toitsu-do is ideal for fashioning an environment that encourages examination of the real character of the universe, the self, and the Way. To help actualize such an environment, you can try anjo daza ho or muga ichi-nen ho before more physical aspects of study. And while practicing, take note of whether or not the relative, personal self is forgotten, and also whether the present moment and the immediate environment pervades your awareness.

Lapses in mind and body harmony can be detected by way of "body language." If your psychophysical posture is unbalanced, your exercises will also lack balance. What does your posture say about you? This not to propose that you should become self-conscious while training your mind and body—awareness and self-consciousness are not the same.

Enjoy your practice, but don't drop the meditative state when your training session is completed. Take it into ordinary life, and use it to benefit yourself and others. To help you accomplish this, you may also want to close your practice with anjo daza ho or muga ichi-nen ho.

HARA: "abdomen." Concentrating psychophysical energy in the lower abdomen is one of the hallmarks of Nakamura Sensei's Japanese yoga. When attention is centered at a point below the navel, it's natural for action to originate from this location. Because our hara area encompasses some of our largest muscles and occupies our physcial center, it is essential for coordinating the movement of the upper and lower body.

Chapter 7
YODO HO PSYCHOPHYSICAL EXERCISES

FIVE PRINCIPLES FOR YODO HO

1. Relax the shoulders.

2. Do not let any part of the body, particularly the anus, become limp.

3. Concentrate ki at the natural center in the lower hara.

4. Find and maintain the most comfortable rhythm.

5. Think that your hara's motion becomes infinitely small.

While training the mind is essential, a powerful mind in a weak, diseased, or uncoordinated body can't express itself easily. As a result, Nakamura Sensei taught *yodo ho.*

Yodo ho is a unique series of exercises that can be practiced when standing, squatting, sitting, or reclining and that function as both meditation and health maintenance. Yo means "to foster, cultivate, or develop," while *do,* in this case, indicates "movement." *Ho,* as you'll recall from previous chapters, is simply a "method" or "exercise." The term was designed to describe a kind of movement that aids in the development of the mind and body.

That rhythmic movement should relate to the mind isn't as strange as it might seem. All over the world, children (and sometimes adults) will rock back and forth rhythmically when they're deeply afraid or when they've suffered great psychological trauma. This rhythmic action is an automatic, spontaneous reaction designed to calm and stabilize the nervous system. It seems to be an innate response in human beings. I feel that the origins of yodo ho lie in this innate reflex.

Nakamura Tempu Sensei taught that the benefits of yodo ho include:

- alignment of the internal organs
- improved digestion
- improved circulation of blood
- a balanced distribution of ki to every part of the body
- alignment of the spine and improved posture
- gentle exercise for inactive people or individuals in poor health
- a calming influence on the nervous system
- a means to discover the nature of perseverance and spiritual strength

Yodo ho can be practiced in four positions. You can choose the posture that's most convenient for a given set of circumstances or that will aid you in developing a particular part of your body, or you can practice the four postures as an integrated series of progressive, related movements.

Fig. 11. Tatte Suru Yodo Ho. While standing, raise your heels and let your knees bend slightly. Begin and maintain a rhythmic up-and-down movement of your body.

For example, if you're outdoors, lying down might not be ideal, but standing would work well. If you're interested in improving the alignment of your vertebrae, the reclining position offers more than the standing posture. If you're more concerned with calming the mind as opposed to exercising the body, seated yodo ho is less strenuous.

Tatte Suru Yodo Ho

Tatte suru yodo ho is the standing form of yodo ho (Figure 11). Interlace your fingers as in anjo daza ho and place them against your hara so that your little-finger edges touch your abdomen about four finger widths below the navel. Your feet are shoulder width apart, with the toes pointing a bit outward.

Raise your heels and let your knees bend slightly. Then, start a rhythmic up-and-down movement of your body so that your heels strike the ground. The impact isn't too heavy, but rather just enough to send a gentle vibration through the body. A jarring collision only places us in conflict with nature and indicates a movement that's too tense and forced or too limp and sagging. Both are ineffective in terms of mind and body coordination.

Focus your attention on the movement of your hara—all action in yodo ho originates from this point. This focusing also brings the mind into the moment.

Find a comfortable rhythm and continue as long as you can. Don't strain. This form of yodo ho limbers and strengthens your toes, feet, ankles, and calves. Your calves in particular will rapidly feel the effects of this exercise. To keep your legs and calves more relaxed, let your knees flex as you move. If your calf muscles grow tired too rapidly, try bending your knees a bit more for awhile. In essence, vary the amount of bend in your knees to vary the amount of stress on your calves.

In time, everyone grows fatigued. At that moment, let the up and down movement of your hara gradually decrease, with the feeling that this movement continues infinitely smaller.

Shagande Suru Yodo Ho

Shagande suru yodo ho is the squatting form of yodo ho. It loosens and strengthens the knees and thighs. Tension in the lower back is released as well. We can discover a heightened sense of balance through this exercise.

Correct posture is vital for balance here. Keep your upper body perpendicular to the earth, your thighs roughly parallel to the ground,

Fig. 12. Shagande Suru Yodo Ho. Squat with your knees open and your fingers interlaced. Begin and maintain a rhythmic up-and-down movement of your body.

and your heels off the floor. Let your knees open somewhat, and place your interlaced fingers in the same position as tatte suru yodo ho.

Some Westerners find this position difficult to adopt. If your knees are too high you'll end up placing your hands above your navel, which focuses the subconscious at too high a point on the body. In this case, just rest your separated hands or forearms lightly on your knees.

Now, begin a small, gentle, up and down movement originating in your hara as in Figure 12. Sustain this even, rhythmic motion as long as you can comfortably do so. Then, let the motion of your hara grow smaller with a feeling of infinite reduction.

If you have trouble balancing, make sure you drop your shoulders with the thought of settling your upper body weight down into your hara. You can also try focusing your mind on a point lower than four finger widths below the bellybutton. The lower the center of gravity the more stable the object. Your spine's position is also related to stability and balance. Too straight and you'll tip over. Too rounded off (slumped), and you'll wobble. Try to find a balanced posture that's not tense or limp. If need be, initially rest your hand against a wall to stabilize yourself.

Suwatte Suru Yodo Ho

Suwatte suru yodo ho is the seated form of yodo ho. It's ideal for meditation, and it relaxes and strengthens the abdomen, waist, and lower back. It also massages and increases blood circulation to the internal organs.

As in anjo daza ho and muga ichi-nen ho, you can either sit in seiza, *kekka fuza* (full lotus), *hanka fuza* (half-lotus), or *agura* (cross-legged). Using a firm chair is also a possibility, but seiza seems to be most easily utilized.

Sitting lightly, place your hands against your hara as in the two previous positions. Take a look at the posture shown in Figure 13. Focus attention on your hara, and start to move it in a small, clockwise circle. Keep your forehead and lower abdomen aligned as before, and move the rest of the body in conjunction with your hara. Your body movement is stemming from your hara and not your head, which is only along for the ride.

When you wish to stop, don't do so abruptly, but rather, move in an infinitely decreasing spiral. Even when the body movement is no longer visible, you should have the sensation of this motion continuing internally forever.

Make sure that you return to your original, aligned posture. You

Fig. 13. Suwatte Suru Yodo Ho. Sit with your hands placed against your hara. Focus attention on your hara, and move it in a small, clockwise circle, then stop it by moving in a decreasing spiral. The sensation is of this motion continuing internally forever. Return to your original posture.

shouldn't be sitting either in a swaybacked manner or with an outward curve in the lumbar vertebrae.

Gyoga Shite Suru Yodo Ho

Gyoga shite suru yodo ho is the reclining form. It exercises the whole body from the shoulders to the feet. It also increases the flexibility of the back, aligns the spine, and strengthens the back muscles.

Your feet are shoulder width apart. Place your hands behind your head. These two points are designed to stabilize the upper and lower parts of your body. Don't move your head and shoulders or your feet during this exercise.

Raise your hips slightly so that they can slide sideways easily across the ground. Move your hara from side to side, parallel to the

Fig. 14. Gyoga Shite Suru Yodo Ho. Place your hands behind your head and move your hara from side to side. Continue until you're tired and then decrease the motion.

floor. Make the movement as large as is comfortable. It resembles the swaying motion of a swimming fish. As before, continue until you're tired, then begin a gradually decreasing motion that grows endlessly smaller (Figure 14).

Raising your hips too high in this exercise will cause excessive strain. On the other hand, if it feels like you may start a fire with the friction of your rear end, you probably need to lighten up. Experiment to find the proper posture.

Your mind is centered on the hara as before, but in this case, your apex of concentration isn't on the front surface of the lower abdomen but rather toward the spine (due to gravity). Settle your mind at this point, keeping it in the present moment.

Important Points

Listed at the beginning of this chapter are the five main points for performing yodo ho. These points are essential, for without them, we're really only wiggling around. With them, virtually any form of natural and rhythmic movement can be yodo ho.

Here's a quick story to illustrate the last statement. Travel in Tokyo and other large Japanese cities frequently takes place on packed subway trains where having to stand in the aisle is common.

These crowded trains sway quite a bit as they wind their way through the subterranean tunnels, forcing most people to hold onto overhead handles, seats, or some other objects to stabilize themselves. When I first met Hashimoto Tetsuichi Sensei, we hopped a train to visit Tempu-kai ("The Tempu Society"), the Japanese headquarters of Nakamura Tempu Sensei's organization. I noticed that even though he was standing, Hashimoto Sensei made no attempt to hold onto anything. He never lost his balance even as the train lurched, swayed, stopped, and started without warning. His feet were immovable, never shuffling an inch to regain equilibrium. Instead, his body swayed from the hara, coordinating with the subway's rhythm.

I tried copying him, with some success. And yet, despite previous training in Shin-shin-toitsu-do combined with decades of martial arts practice, I still was unable to prevent my feet from shuffling occasionally to keep from stumbling. Hashimoto Sensei caught me looking at him and, with a wink, made a simple statement, "Davey-san, yodo ho."

This scenario would repeat itself over the years, with Hashimoto Sensei explaining that not only was yodo ho the key to his remarkable art of "subway surfing," but that he was in fact practicing yodo ho itself as his body moved rhythmically in the aisle of the wobbling train. To him, any movement performed with a natural, relaxed rhythm and unification of mind and body was yodo ho.

Thus, the principles are more important than the specifics. However, we need to discover this ourselves.

As you practice any version of yodo ho, your shoulders must be relaxed. This allows your weight to sink down to your hara, resulting in exceptional balance. Try swinging your arms back and forth and then let their movement gradually grow smaller, until your arms are still. Don't force your arms to stop, but relax fully so that their arc grows progressively smaller on its own. This is an excellent way to release tension in the arms and the shoulders, and it can be done before performing yodo ho or any other action.

While you want to drop and relax your shoulders, you also want to avoid falling limp. Stand, squat, sit, or lie down with a light feeling. In standing, avoid being flat-footed or resting on your heels. With the weight on the balls of your feet, place your heels lightly on the ground.

In seiza, rest your buttocks gently on your heels as well. Avoid plopping down heavily onto your feet because this will lead to a basically negative, nonfunctional form of relaxation.

Squat with a light feeling. Your body shouldn't droop limply toward the earth, and your lower back shouldn't slump. In every case, try for the feeling of being suspended between heaven and earth—neither sagging toward the ground nor pressing upward toward heaven. Simply float.

In reclining, again, avoid flopping down onto the ground as if your body were lifeless. Place yourself gently on the ground as you would a glass filled with water onto a table. If you plop the glass down, you'll cause it to clatter against the table and spill its contents. To keep your body filled with ki, lay it down lightly on the floor in a similar manner.

All of these ideas relate to an attitude that is balanced between tension and collapse. And all relate to the posture of kumbhaka, so you might want to review Chapter 4.

THE HARA AND RHYTHM

If your attention is centered at a point below the navel, it's natural for action to originate from this center.

Since our hara area encompasses some of the largest muscles in the body, and because it's the midpoint of the body, this point is essential for coordinating the movement of the upper and lower body. It also relates to fostering mind and body coordination. However, creating a sort of "tunnel vision" in which we attempt to block everything out but this abdominal point is impractical and even claustrophobic. Whatever we practice should be applicable universally in life. If the mind concentrates on one thing exclusively, it cannot effectively think of anything else. Yet if the mind divides itself, no real concentration takes place.

Hashimoto Sensei [explained] that not only was yodo bo the key to his remarkable art of "subway surfing," but that he was in fact practicing yodo bo itself as his body moved rhythmically in the aisle of the wobbling train.

Our natural center in the lower hara is not separate from everything else and neither are we. Think of the center hole in a doughnut. Can we separate the doughnut hole and the rest of the doughnut? No hole, no doughnut. No doughnut, no hole.

In short, when the mind focuses at this center in the lower

abdomen, it also becomes aware of everything surrounding this point, creating oneness. Once this condition is attained, simply keep the mind concentrated on what's taking place in the present, which is the rhythmic movement of your hara. It's a relaxed concentration.

What's the most comfortable rhythm? We need to find this since yodo ho involves not merely rhythmic action, but *relaxed* movement. What is comfortable varies from person to person and from moment to moment. (One day it might feel better to move quickly. Another day, depending on your mental and physical state, a slower rhythm may be more relaxing.)

Taking this into account, we must allow the mind to rest in the instant, continually discovering the most comfortable rhythm. The constant discovery of the ever-changing moment is concentration.

The most comfortable rhythm cannot be given to you, but it can be found. Once it's found, it should be sustained. Erratic rhythm isn't as relaxing as a smooth, even rhythm. We break the rhythm when our attention is broken or our body tightens—when ki stops. Ki will stop when the mind gets stuck on any action, desire, or fear.

Our universe is alive. Being alive it's filled with continual change and constant movement of ki. I used to comment that only dead things fail to move, and as ki amounts to living energy, it must remain in motion. But actually, a dead body decomposes and continues to change form. *Nothing* is static. To cling to thoughts, feelings, people, the past—anything—is to fight against the natural rhythmic movement of ki in the universe.

Consequently, two points are important: discovering the most natural rhythm, and noticing breaks in this rhythm that essentially equate to breaks in mind-body coordination and ki movement.

SUGGESTIONS FOR PRACTICING YODO HO

All of these exercises are gentle, making them ideal for people in poor health. Still, most of us want to strengthen our bodies and improve our health. To accomplish this, slowly increase the amount of time you spend on each exercise. While the standing form of yodo ho is easy enough that virtually anyone can perform it immediately, even healthy people may find their calves giving out after just 5 minutes of sus-tained action. Therefore, yodo ho is soft enough for the elderly and infirm to begin yet powerful enough to present a real challenge to the muscles of healthy people. To build up the various parts of the body that are affected by each yodo ho posture, don't put more force in the movements or unnat-urally speed up, just increase the amount of time you perform each one. Gradually, without forcing, lengthen each session. Our bodies, espe-cially the legs, can be built up easily and safely in this way.

Our natural center in the lower hara is not separate from everything else and neither are we. Think of the center hole in a doughnut. Can we separate the doughnut hole and the rest of the doughnut? No hole, no doughnut. No doughnut, no hole.

We tend to use our legs more than most parts of the body. Even sitting in a chair while reading this book, your body weight is still pressed down on your legs. Perhaps only while lying flat on the back are the legs completely free from stress. When animals and people become elderly or ill, the first thing to go is the legs. You know you're really sick when you can't stand or walk, and in this sense the legs are the underpinning of the whole body. The older we get the more impor-tant balance and this bodily foundation become.

If we follow the sequence of movements outlined above, we'll first exercise the feet, ankles, and calves, followed by the knees and thighs, then the waist, abdomen, and lower back, then finally the upper back and most of the body. Nearly all of the body is exercised systematically and simply, from the ground up, ending in a position that's ideal for resting.

How should the body eventually come to rest in each posture? We've already noted that rhythmic movement is relaxing, so avoid an abrupt stop that would break this feeling of composure. Instead, while your mind continues to follow the movement of your hara, gradually make this movement smaller, smaller, smaller. . . . No matter how small it becomes, something will always be left—the process of reduction is infinite. The sensation of calmness can also be sustained endlessly. And as the mind is focused on this reducing motion, its own movement grows smaller, moving toward an action that's infinitely smaller and infinitely more rapid.

For instance, it takes less time to move 6 inches than to move 12 inches. And it takes even less time to move 3 inches than it does to move 6 inches. Thus, as the movement of the hara reduces, it also becomes faster, until its movement is so fast that it can't be seen or felt. Anything that is truly still is also truly rapid.

As a result, ancient Asian meditation texts have mentioned a state of "stillness in motion, motion in stillness." As we keep the mind calm at the natural center in the lower abdomen during yodo ho, we demonstrate "stillness in motion." Then, when we begin to reduce this yodo ho movement to an endlessly small point, we arrive at "motion in stillness." In other words, when we can no longer see the reducing movement of the body, we should do nothing and let this process of infinite reduction continue to vibrate within us. This is the physical equivalent of following the endlessly reducing waves of sound in anjo daza ho. Both exercises lead to calmness via different applications of the same principle. Despite the fact that some practitioners of Shin-shin-toitsu-do cease yodo ho suddenly and immediately go onto something else after the physical motion stops, this kind of training amounts to only one half of the equation. Letting the movement of ki continue infinitely smaller, although all outward action has ceased, is valuable. Try using (for example) 5 minutes of movement followed by an equal 5 minutes of being outwardly motionless.

The words "stillness in motion, motion in stillness" are easy to read. Let's try using yodo ho as a tool to discover their real meaning as well as the nature of genuine calmness in the midst of an active life.

SHOMETSU: "life/death, appearance/disappearance," painted in the semi-cursive gyosho style of the famed calligrapher Ogishi. Nakamura Sensei considered functioning in the instant, while transcending any thought of living and dying, to be a central pillar of Shin-shin-toitsu-do. In the instant, past, present, and future are one, as are living and dying.

Chapter 8

HITORI RYOHO SELF-HEALING

FIVE PRINCIPLES FOR HITORI RYOHO
---
1. Find the posture of mind and body unification.

2. As you move, do not lose this unified posture.

3. When using yuki, remember the principles for the transmission of ki.

4. Do not force the body to respond.

5. Spend extra time on weak areas and practice regularly.

H*itori* means "by yourself," or "individual," and *ryoho* indicates a "healing art." What follows are methods to increase blood circulation to body parts, promote flexibility, aid in relaxation, and enhance the movement of ki. Like yodo ho, these healing arts are important for unification of mind and body in daily life. A tense, unhealthy body isn't capable of responding to even the most concentrated mind.

To accomplish the above objectives, we can massage the body through tapping and rubbing actions. We can also promote flexibility via calisthenics-type movements and stretching. Most importantly, we

179

can directly send ki to different parts of the body by pressing with the fingertips and focusing the mind on this "injection of ki" (*yuki*).

Consider your car. It runs by means of its battery and electrical energy. If the battery grows weak, we use jumper cables to transmit electricity to it—we jump-start the battery. When performing yuki, think of your hands and fingers as the jumper cables. Transfusion of ki to various body parts can be compared to a blood transfusion (*yuketsu*) or a jump-start. Visualizing the transfusion of ki is a useful aid.

Over the span of Nakamura Sensei's life he continued to modify these healing arts (and other aspects of Shin-shin-toitsu-do). As a result, more than one version of these techniques exists. Maintaining health is the main objective of these exercises. In other words, they amount to preventive medicine. They can also be used to aid in recovery from injury or illness and to treat other people.

1. Arm Rotation Exercise

Raise one arm overhead without lifting the shoulder unnaturally. Relax your hand, arm, and wrist. Then, let your arm (*ude*) fall downward and swing back overhead again in a narrow, vertical oval as in Figure 15. Do not make a wide, round circle, but instead allow your arm to drop straight down of its own accord. You can swing the arm backward or forward. Due to the power of reaction, if you continue to relax, your arm will swing up again pretty much by itself. Focus your attention on the descending action. Think of a traditional rollercoaster. As you go down, it speeds up. When you start to go uphill, the car gradually slows, pausing slightly at the top before regaining momentum as the car moves rapidly down the next slope. Use a similar

Fig. 15. Arm Rotation Exercise. Raise one arm overhead, without lifting the shoulder. Let the arm fall and swing back overhead again.

natural rhythm to arrive at relaxation and mind-body coordination in this exercise.

The arm rotation movement loosens the shoulders and enhances the circulation of blood. It's designed to prevent or alleviate stiff shoulders and tension-related headaches. Repeat as much as is comfortable and necessary. Practice equally on both the right and left sides. This advice holds true for the following exercises as well.

This is a simplified version of the arm rotation exercise. It's possible but more difficult to move both arms at once or alternatingly.

2. Shoulder Therapy

Make a loose fist by tucking your thumb inside the fingers of your hand. Reach across to the opposite shoulder and place your fist about 8

Fig. 16. Shoulder Therapy. Tuck your thumb inside the fingers of your hand and reach across to the opposite shoulder. Drop the flat part of your fist onto the shoulder. Relax. Tap along the length of the shoulder in a slow rhythm. Avoid lifting and tensing the shoulders or arms.

to 12 inches above the shoulder muscles (Figure 16). Then, concentrating your attention on the downward movement, drop your fist palm-side down onto the shoulder (*kata*). If you relax completely, your fist will rise again by itself, and you can repeat the action once more. Continue to tap along the length of the shoulder, loosening the muscles. Then repeat for the other shoulder. (Some of Nakamura Sensei's students alternate tapping from one shoulder to the other, but this is a bit more difficult.) Use a slow, relaxed rhythm. A steady, calm rhythm itself helps promote relaxation. Aim for about one downward movement per second, similar to 4/4 time in music.

Avoid lifting and tensing the shoulders or arms. Don't beat yourself up either. Great force is actually counterproductive. Use this exercise longer and more frequently to relax particularly tense shoulders and promote blood circulation.

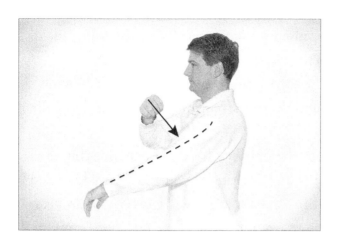

Fig. 17. Arm Therapy. Tuck your thumb inside your fingers and form a loose fist. Place the fist over your arm and let it fall to tap the back of the arm. Using the flat of the palm side of your fist, work your way from the top to the bottom of the arm. Repeat.

You can use this and other hitori ryoho exercises in the morning to start the day in a positive way. You can also perform them before sleep to relax the mind and body so you fall asleep more readily. And they can be used during the day as well. In fact, this exercise may be useful for people whose shoulders become tired from spending many hours sitting in front of a computer.

3. Arm Therapy

Next, we'll work on the arms. We start with exercises that relax the shoulders, arms, wrists, and fingers because we'll be using the hands and fingertips to transmit ki in the subsequent drills. Transmission of life energy is most easily accomplished in a state of relaxation.

Tuck your thumb inside your fingers again to form a loose fist. Hold it over your opposite arm, then let it fall to tap the back of your arm as in Figure 17. You're doing to the arm what you did to the shoulders in exercise 2, above. Use the same loose wrist and relaxed rhythm, letting the weight of your arm drop to the underside. Remember to

183

focus on the downward movements and use the flat of the palm side of your fist. Avoid hitting with the sharp angles of the finger joints.

Work your way from the top to the bottom of your arm repeatedly. Next, turn your arm over and do the same thing to the inside of the arm (Figure 18).

Now, grip your arm with the opposite hand so that your thumb is on the underside of your arm and the tips of your index, middle, and ring fingers are touching the top of your arm. See Figure 19 for an illustration. Press your fingers down your arm along the line (*suji*) running from your shoulder to your middle finger.

Align the three fingertips so they form an even surface without the longer middle finger sticking out and applying most of the pressure. Then, using a relaxed, squeezing action, press firmly into the muscles of your arm with your fingertips. A sharp but not excessively painful sensation should be produced. Hold this pressure steadily while visualizing a stream of ki flowing from your fingertips into your arm (as in the orenai te exercise discussed in Chapter 3). You can decide how long to sustain the pressure. Generally, 30 seconds in each spot is good. And while some of Nakamura Sensei's students use a quicker action, it seems ki is more effectively transmitted, and deeper muscle relaxation achieved, if you press longer in each place.

It's important not to assume that we've mastered anything and to rediscover the posture and attitude of mind and body unity from moment to moment. Life is now in session . . . are we present?

Finally, flip your arm over and press with the fingertips along a line running from the shoulder over your biceps and down your forearm to your middle finger. As before, keep your thumb on the underside of the

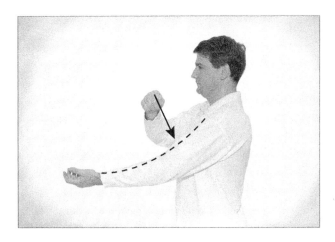

Fig. 18. Tap along the inside of the arm, working your way from top to bottom.

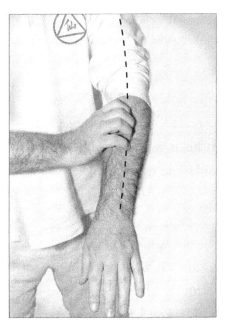

Fig. 19. Press down a line running from the shoulder to the middle finger, along the back of the arm. Press firmly into the muscles and produce a sharp, but not painful, sensation. As you hold this pressure, visualize ki flowing from the fingertips into the arm. Press each spot for about 30 seconds.

arm, and apply a penetrating, squeezing action while thinking of directing ki from your fingertips into the arm muscles as in Figure 20. Stay in each spot for roughly 30 seconds, and work down to the wrist. Always treat both arms equally.

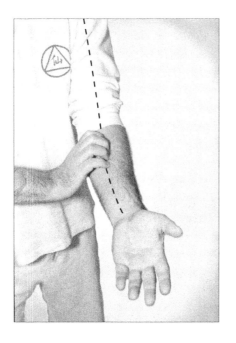

Fig. 20. Flip your arm over and press with the fingertips along a line running from the shoulder, over the biceps, and down the forearm to the middle finger. As you apply a penetrating, squeezing action, think of directing ki from your fingertips into the arm. Stay in each spot for roughly 30 seconds, and work down to the wrist.

These arm-therapy techniques were created to soften tense muscles, stimulate nerves and blood vessels in the arms, and promote overall relaxation. Most significantly, they stimulate ki in the arms.

4. Wrist Exercise

The following wrist exercises, or *tekubi no undo*, are great for improving circulation and flexibility in the joints of the wrists and fingers. Hold your arms and wrists as in Figure 21 and move your wrists from side to side loosely without moving your forearms and elbows. Make a quick, relaxed movement, as if drawing a level arc from side to side with your fingertips. Point the fingertips inward and then outward quickly with a sort of shaking action.

Now, keeping the arms in the same position, flap your wrists up

Fig. 21. Wrist Exercise. Move your wrists from side to side loosely as your forearms and elbows remain still. Draw a level arc from side to side; point your fingertips inward and then outward quickly, with a shaking action.

Fig. 22. Now flap your wrists up and down. Relax and draw an up/down vertical arc with the fingertips. Shake the wrists quickly and freely.

and down (Figure 22). Relax the wrists and rapidly draw an up and down, vertical arc with the fingertips so that the fingers first point up and then down. Shake the wrists quickly and freely.

Still keeping your arms in the same position, repeatedly draw clockwise circles with your fingertips. Then, draw counterclockwise circles. Make these circles as large as possible without moving the arms as in Figure 23. This holds true for the previous wrist exercises as well.

Next, raise your arms overhead, then open and close your hands

Fig. 23. Keeping your arms in the same position as before, draw clockwise and counter-clockwise circles with your fingertips.

repeatedly. Open the fingers as widely as possible, and then make a fist.

Fig. 24. With arms overhead, open the fingers wide and make a fist. Repeat several times. Then shake your wrists and fingers.

Do this quickly to exercise the fingers, hands, and wrists. Continue until you feel tired, then shake your wrists and fingers vigorously in all directions while still holding your arms overhead (Figure 24). Imagine you have gum on your fingers and you're trying to shake it loose. When you feel tired, drop your arms.

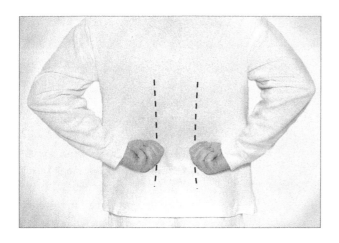

Fig. 25. Back Therapy. Make a loose fist with your thumbs tucked inside your fingers. Tap down a line of muscle along each side of the spine, from as high as you can reach and down to the hips.

5. Back Therapy

Tuck your thumbs inside your fingers to form loose fists as before. Using the thumb side of both fists, tap down the line of muscle running along each side of your spine (Figure 25). This line is about two finger widths from the spine and feels like a large cord running under the skin. Start at the top, as high as you can reach in a relaxed manner, and work down to the hipbone. Use the same tapping action as before, but make contact with the thumb side of the loose fist.

Now, using the tips of both thumbs, press into the same band of muscle. Whenever you apply yuki pressure with the fingertips, press in until your fingers stop naturally, and then just hold the pressure. As you project ki, you may find that the tissue softens, allowing you to press more deeply. Don't force, but do press in fully until the fingertips stop naturally.

Create a penetrating feeling, and hold the pressure for 30 seconds in each spot. As you sustain pressure, visualize ki flowing into your back (se) from your thumbs. Start as high as you can comfortably

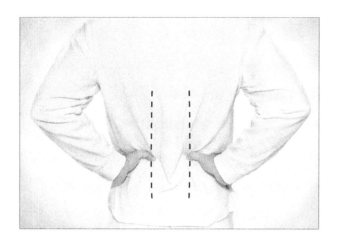

Fig. 26. Use both thumbs to press into the muscle along each side of the spine. Press until the fingers stop, then hold for 30 seconds in each spot. Start high and work down to the hips.

reach, and work your way down to the hips, stimulating ki in the lumbar area (Figure 26). If you find a particularly stiff or painful place, stay there longer.

Quite a few people have lower back problems, usually stemming from lack of exercise and poor posture. This book may be useful for people with back problems since it addresses both exercise and posture. What's more, this specific exercise may be especially helpful in alleviating and/or preventing lower back pain and stiffness.

6. *Side of the Body Therapy*

Place the palms on the sides of your torso (*taisokubu*) as in Figure 27. Keeping your elbows back and pointed to the rear, rub the sides of your body with a rapid and vigorous up and down action. Continue until this area feels hot.

This exercise stimulates the skin, relaxes the side muscles, and promotes blood circulation.

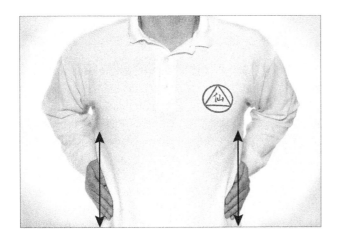

Fig. 27. Side of the Body Therapy. Use your palms to rub the sides of your body with a vigorous up/down action.

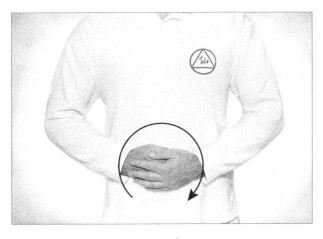

Fig. 28. Abdominal Therapy. With your hands atop each other, rub your abdomen in a large clockwise circle around the navel.

7. Abdominal Therapy

Put your right palm on your abdomen and cover it with your left palm. Pressing in slightly, rub energetically in a fairly large clockwise circle around your navel (Figure 28). Use quick circles, over and over, until the abdominal area (*fukubu*) becomes hot.

This rubbing action enhances blood circulation to the skin and abdomen, relaxes the muscles in the torso, and benefits the internal

Fig. 29. Eye Therapy. Close your eyes. Rub from the tear duct outward, and reverse. Next rub downward, past the eyelashes, and then upward in reverse. Finally, with index, middle, and ring fingers together, touch a line across the center of the eyelids. Touch softly as you send ki from the fingers into the eyes.

organs as well. This exercise may also improve digestion because the intestines are affected.

8. Eye Therapy

Shin-shin-toitsu-do practitioners commonly use the following method to alleviate eyestrain. Again, your aim is to enhance the circulation of blood and ki as well as to promote relaxation.

Close your eyes and begin by using the flat part of your fingers to gently rub from the tear duct outward as in Figure 29. Repeat this soft, wiping action going in one direction from the inside out, not back and forth.

Next, reverse your movement and wipe from the outside corner of your eye inward toward your nose and tear duct. Don't use your fingertips but instead make contact with the flat part of your fingers.

Third, rub downward from the top of your eye, down past the eyelashes. Again, use the flat of your fingers and go in only one direction—downward. Repeat as often as is comfortable.

Fig. 30. Eye Exercise. Face forward, hands on hips. The head and body do not move. Look upward as far as you can. Hold for 2 seconds, then look downward and hold. Repeat several times. Then look far to the left without moving the head. Hold. Look far to the right. Hold. Finally, move your eyes slowly in large clockwise and counterclockwise circles.

Fourth, reverse the above motion, and rub upward, repeatedly moving from the bottom of your eyes toward the eyebrows.

And fifth, make the tips of your index, middle, and ring fingers even with each other. Close your eyes, and touch the line running across the center of the eyelids with your fingertips. Just touch softly, without much pressure, and concentrate on sending ki from the fingers into the eyes (*gankyu*). About 30 seconds should be enough.

9. Eye Exercise

This is an eye exercise, or *gankyu undo*, that's designed to strengthen the eyes. Students report this exercise is also helpful for relieving eyestrain.

Place your hands on your hips and face forward. Without moving your head, look upward as far as possible, as in Figure 30. Hold for about 2 seconds, then look downward as far as you can and hold for 2 seconds. Repeat several times.

Then, look as far to the left as you can without moving your head.

Fig. 31. Nose Therapy. Place your fingers together. Pull your thumbs inside and point them toward the middle of the palms. Using the sides of your index fingers, rub vigorously along the sides of the nose and the cheeks.

Hold this position a few seconds, then look as far to the right as possible. Hold. Repeat several times.

Last, move your eyes slowly in a large clockwise circle several times, and then form several counterclockwise circles. In every case, don't move your head or body.

10. Nose Therapy

Open your hands, make your fingers straight, and place them together. Tuck your thumb inside, pointing it toward the middle of your palm. Then, using the sides of your index fingers, rub repeatedly and vigorously along the sides of the nose (*hana*) and the cheek area near it (Figure 31). Continue until this area feels hot.

Your goal is to release tension and promote blood circulation. Several of my students have indicated that this method has provided relief from sinus congestion.

Fig. 32. Mouth and Gum Therapy. Put your fingers together and spread your thumb. Place the web of your thumb between your upper lip and the base of your nose.

Fig. 33. Now form your other hand into the same shape and place the thumb web below the lower lip.

11. Mouth and Gum Therapy

Put your straightened fingers together and open your thumb. Then place the web of your thumb between your upper lip and the base of your nose as in Figure 32. Next, form the same shape with your other hand, and place the thumb web right below the lower lip as in Figure 33.

Now, move your hands in opposite directions, from side to side, to

Fig. 34. Move both hands side to side in opposite directions until the gums, lips, and mouth feel hot and tingly.

rub against your gums. Rub repeatedly until your gums, lips, and mouth feel hot and tingly (Figure 34).

Your objective is to strengthen and stimulate the flow of blood to the gum area (*haguki*).

12. Facial Therapy

Place the palms of both hands on the surface of your face and cheeks (*ganmen*) as in Figure 35. Rub energetically up and down until the face feels hot. As you move, sustain a relaxed and centered condition that maintains coordination of mind and body. In this state of mind and body unification, you'll naturally transmit ki from your palms as you treat yourself. This is true for all of the above and subsequent techniques.

Your face will become red from the enhanced circulation of blood. The generated warmth and massaging action releases tension in the facial muscles and vitalizes the skin and facial nerves.

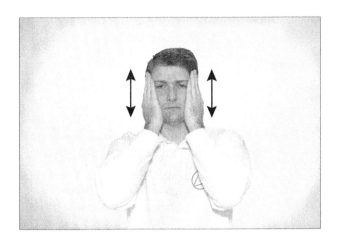

Fig. 35. Facial Therapy. Place your palms on your face and cheeks. Rub up and down until your face feels hot.

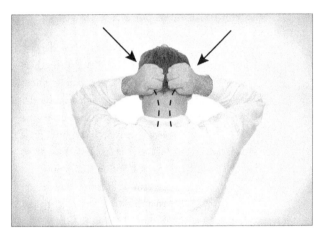

Fig. 36. Back of the Neck and Base of the Skull Therapy. Form loose fists with your thumbs inside your fingers. Tap repeatedly around the base of the skull and then down the muscles along the sides of the cervical vertebrae.

13. Back of the Neck and Base of the Skull Therapy

Place your thumbs inside your fingers to form loose fists. Using the flat, palm side of your fists, tap repeatedly around the base of the skull (*kotobu*) as in Figure 36. Following this, tap down the muscles that run along the sides of your spine (cervical vertebrae) in the neck area (*keibu*). Do this several times as well. The objective is to release tension in the neck muscles and promote circulation.

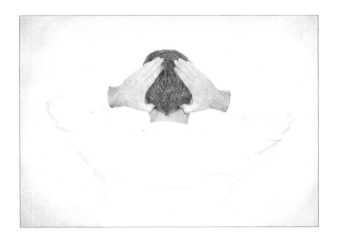

Fig. 37. Hook the tips of your thumbs under the base of the skull near your ears. Press in and up under the base of the skull with your thumbs. Hold for 30 seconds and work in toward the spine.

Fig. 38. With the middle fingers of both hands together, touch the indentation where the top of the spine meets the base of the skull. Lean the head and neck slightly back against your fingers, press inward, and mentally project a stream of ki from your fingertips that travels parallel to the ground.

Now, place your fingertips on top of your skull, and hook the tips of your thumbs under the base of your skull near your ears (Figure 37). Press in and up under the base of your skull with your thumbs, mentally directing a stream of ki toward your forehead. Lean your head slightly to the rear. Aim for a sharp, penetrating sensation, and stay in each location for around 30 seconds as you work your way in toward your spine. (Do not apply pressure to your spine in this or any other form of hitori ryoho.) My students have used this technique to alleviate

Fig. 39. Salivary Gland Stimulation. Place three fingers of both hands evenly together and touch in front of the lower ear and near the hinge of the jaw. Press in firmly for about 30 seconds.

or prevent headaches. The upward movement of ki also affects the brain.

Last, place the middle fingers of both hands together, and touch the spot (known as *bon no kubo*) where the top of the spine meets the base of the skull (Figure 38). Search for what feels like an indentation. Then, leaning your head and neck slightly back against your fingers, press inward and mentally project a stream of ki from your fingertips that travels parallel to the ground (not at an upward angle). This stimulates the base of the brain and may also be useful in dealing with headaches.

14. Salivary Gland Stimulation

The following techniques are designed to stimulate the production of saliva and strengthen the salivary glands (*bunpisen*). Increased production of saliva benefits the throat and voice and also aids digestion.

First, placing the three fingers of both hands evenly together as in exercise 3 (arm therapy), touch the area in front of your lower ear and

Fig. 40. Press the tips of your thumbs into the soft tissue along the inside edge of the jawbone. Begin at the top of the jaw and move down to the underside of the chin, staying in each spot for 30 seconds.

near the hinge of your jaw (Figure 39). Press in firmly and send ki from your fingertips for about 30 seconds.

Second, use the tips of your thumbs to press into the soft tissue along the inside edge of your jawbone. Starting at the top of your jaw (Figure 40), create a sharp sensation for 30 seconds in each spot while visualizing ki flowing into the body. Work your way down to the underside of your chin. Your thumbs should be touching each other, side by side, at this final location. You are not pressing on your jawbone or chin itself, but rather, into the soft tissue alongside the bone. Press with the ball of your thumb, but don't stand the finger on end so that the nail digs uncomfortably into the skin. This is good advice for any form of energy transference using the fingertips.

Third, with the thumb and fingers of the right hand, touch the line that runs along the side of your windpipe (Figure 41). Using the flat part of your fingers, rub up and down on your throat to stimulate circulation of blood.

Fourth, using your right thumb and fingertips, touch the same line between your throat muscles and windpipe, but this time use the tips of

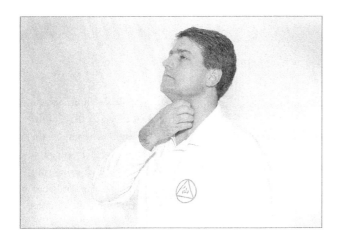

Fig. 41. Use the flat parts of the thumb and fingers of the right hand to touch a line that runs alongside the windpipe. Rub up and down to stimulate blood circulation.

Fig. 42. Use your right finger-tips to touch the line that runs between the throat muscles and the windpipe. Covering the back of your right hand with your left hand, gently pinch with the fingers of the right hand as you press toward the back of the neck with the left hand. Work downward to the base of the throat, staying in each location 30 seconds.

your fingers instead of the flat portion. Cover the back of your right hand with your left hand. Next, pinch gently inward with the fingers of your right hand and press toward the back of your neck with the left hand (Figure 42). Direct ki at a 45-degree angle to the center of your windpipe. Stay in each location 30 seconds as you work downward to the base of your throat.

Last, place three fingers together, and touch the base of the throat, near the hollow of your neck. With your fingertips level to the ground

Fig. 43. With three fingers together, touch the base of the throat near the hollow of the neck. Keep your fingertips level with the ground; using your other hand for added pressure, gently press straight into the throat for 30 seconds.

Fig. 44. Ear Therapy. Place the tips of your middle fingers on the indentation in front of your ear opening. Apply pressure for 30 seconds.

and using your other hand for added pressure, gently press straight into your throat and direct ki to this area for 30 seconds (Figure 43). This affects the thyroid gland.

15. Ear Therapy

The following exercises are designed to maintain hearing and the health of the ears (*mimi*).

Fig. 45. Pull up on the top of your ear with your thumb and index finger. Repeat several times. Then grip the bottom of the ear lobe and pull downward. Repeat. Now pull the side of the ear lobe away from the head; you can also make circles. Pinch the lobes to stimulate nerves and blood vessels.

Place the tips of the middle fingers of each hand in front of your ear opening as in Figure 44. Feel for an indentation or soft spot. Apply pressure and ki straight into this point for 30 seconds.

Next, grip the top of your ear with your thumb and index finger, and pull upward several times. Second, grip the bottom of the ear lobe, as in Figure 45, and pull downward a few times. Third, grip the side of your ear lobe, and pull it out sideways away from the head for several repetitions. You can also move your ears in a circular manner using the same grip. Pinch the ear lobes firmly between the

Deep, calm breathing increases the amount of oxygen in the blood, which has a tranquilizing effect on the body. Complete breathing also more fully eliminates carbon dioxide from our bodies. Since oxygen is needed to sustain the metabolic process in the body's cells, deep breathing enhances metabolism, and it has a beneficial effect on every part of the body— not just the lungs.

fingers to stimulate the nerves and blood vessels. Pull with the feeling of widening the opening of your ear canal and extending your ear lobes.

Fig. 46. Ear Canal Pressure and Base of the Skull Stimulation. Press your palms over your ears and apply pressure for a few seconds; then lift your hands from the ears. Do this three times.

Fig. 47. Upon the third repetition, gently close your eyes and slightly bow your head. Tap with your fingertips on the base of the skull for several seconds. Simultaneously open your eyes and uncover your ears. Lift your arms up over your head, and then in a half-circle down to your hara, where you interlace your fingers, palms down.

16. Ear Canal Pressure and Base of the Skull Stimulation

This exercise aims at affecting the health of the inner ear and eardrum. Adopting the posture shown in Figure 46, firmly press your palms over your ears (*jiko no appaku*). Apply pressure for a few seconds and then completely remove your hands from your ears. This covering of the ears, followed by quick and simultaneous removal of both hands, is performed three times.

Fig. 48. Deep Breathing and Positive Affirmation. Continuing from the last exercise, your fingers are interlaced, palms downward in front of the hara.

On the third repetition, gently close your eyes and slightly bow your head. Then, while you keep your ears covered, tap with your fingertips on the base of the skull as seen in Figure 47. Continue this drumming action (*kotobu no shigeki*) for several seconds.

Then, open your eyes and uncover your ears at the same time. Lift your arms over your head and continue to move them in a half-circle down to your hara, where you interlace your fingers, palms down, in front of your lower abdomen.

Continue with the next exercise from this position.

17. Deep Breathing and Positive Affirmation

With your fingers interlaced in front of the hara, the palms facing downward (Figure 48), inhale through your nose and raise your hands

Fig. 49. Inhale and raise your hands overhead. When your lungs are full, hold your breath at your hara and press upward with your hands to stretch the body.

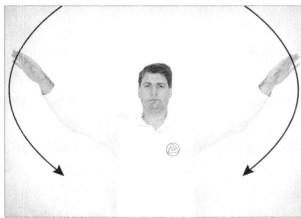

Fig. 50. Next, release the hands. Exhale through your nose as you bring your arms down to the sides to return to the position in Figure 48. Inhale again, through your nose, slowly and evenly. As you inhale, gradually raise your interlaced hands. Pause, hold your breath, and stretch upward.

overhead. When you have inhaled completely, hold your breath at your hara, and press upward with the interlaced hands to stretch your body as in Figure 49 (*nobito shin kokyu*).

Next, release your hands (Figure 50). Very slowly start to exhale through your nose. Aim for a smooth, steady stream of air, and as you exhale, gradually bring your extended arms down to the sides, and then in front of your body to return to the opening position. Inhale again through your nose, but breathe in as slowly as possible, with a constant, even inhalation. As you breathe in, grad-ually raise your linked hands and extended arms in front of your body. At the peak of the inhalation, pause, settling the breath at the hara, and stretch upward. Then, separate your hands, exhaling and lowering your arms to your sides. This deep breathing exercise should be repeated several times.

Breathe purposefully but slowly. Your breathing and body reflect your mind. Just as we want to be relaxed but not limp— and calm but not comatose—our breathing should be not only powerful but slow and calm.

Deep, calm breathing increases the amount of oxygen in the blood, which has a tranquilizing effect on the body. Complete breathing also more fully eliminates carbon dioxide from our bodies. Since oxygen is needed to sustain the metabolic process in the body's cells, deep breath-ing enhances metabolism, and it has a beneficial effect on every part of the body—not just the lungs.

With deeper relaxation comes better circulation of blood, not only to the extremities but to the internal organs. Tension causes the blood vessels to contract, inhibiting circulation. We've all heard the saying that someone got cold feet, meaning they were frightened or nervous. This saying is literally true in that tension affects the circulation of blood to the extremities. Some readers may remember mood rings, which were popular in the 1970s. The stone in the ring would change color to indicate your mood. In reality, the ring was reacting to the warmth or coolness of the hand and fingers. A warm hand equals prop-er circulation, and the stone would turn a color that was claimed to indicate peace of mind or similar qualities. Cold hands produced a change in stone coloration said to signal nervousness or unhappiness—another example of how the body reflects the mind and the effect that relaxation has on the body.

Relaxation aids in full breathing. Deep breathing, when correctly performed, in turn aids in relaxation. Again, due to increased circula-tion of blood throughout the body and a more efficient exchange of oxygen and carbon dioxide in the lungs as well as on a cellular level, this exercise can have a penetrating effect on our overall health. (Even more profound and effective breathing exercises and meditations are found in Shin-shin-toitsu-do, but this must remain the subject of later volumes.)

In connection with this drill, breathe in and out as slowly and calmly as possible, but don't just let the air trickle in and out. Breathe purposefully but slowly. Your breathing and body reflect your mind. Just as we want to be relaxed but not limp—and calm but not comatose—our breathing should be not only powerful but slow and calm.

Actually, while this breathing process is done slowly, it is, even more importantly, extremely deep and full. It sometimes appears to beginners that their teacher is capable of breathing in an inordinately slow manner, but in reality, the teacher is simply breathing in and out more fully than they are. For example, if I use my full lung capacity of 3,000 to 4,000 cc, and you only use 700 cc of your total cubic contents, my breathing will seem to be much slower than yours. It isn't really, but it is much deeper.

So, how can we accomplish a fuller and more profound breathing pattern? This can be achieved in three ways.

First, use the movement of your arms to open and close the chest more completely and thus aid the breathing process. This point is simple and built into the exercise itself.

Second, use positive visualization to help you breathe more deeply. When you inhale, mentally direct the oxygen to your toes and then gradually fill up your entire body as if you were filling a glass with water. Next, when you exhale, imagine the level of air in the body progressively lowering from the top of your head to your neck, then to your hips, and finally back to your toes, until the body is empty. To promote coordination of mind, body, and breath, time your respiration, visualization, and hand movements together. While inhaling and imagining the air filling your body, start to raise your hands when the air level reaches your hara. Move your hands to act as a sort of gauge to show the level of air in your body. Reverse the process for exhaling.

Psychologically speaking, it takes more time to fill the entire body with air than to fill the lungs, which are relatively small by comparison. By using your imagination, you can help yourself to breathe not only more slowly but also more deeply.

And third, the more we relax, the easier it is to breathe fully and calmly. In fact, calm, slow breathing is a reflection of a relaxed state. When we're angry or frightened, our breathing speeds up and becomes rough. When we're peaceful, the process of respiration slows and becomes steady. Breathing practice is, therefore, not only good for the health but also for the mind.

Corresponding to the mind and its powerful effect on the body is the final aspect of hitori ryoho: *kimochi no dantei*. This is a simple positive affirmation done with the eyes closed. An approximate translation of Nakamura Sensei's preferred affirmation is, "My mind and body are moving toward perfect health." Mentally repeat this, or a similar affirmation with full concentration three times at the end of hitori ryoho.

Important Points

Before you begin hitori ryoho—also known as "hitori massage"—it's essential to be in a state of mind and body coordination. If you're not, your body will not follow the dictates of your mind.

This is a state of being that's continually rediscovered. We don't want to "sleepwalk" through life. To avoid this, it's important not to assume that we've mastered anything and to rediscover the posture and attitude of mind and body unity from moment to moment. Life is now in session . . . are we present?

Arriving at this posture isn't the same as sustaining it. Again, we must stay in the moment and notice what's taking place from second to second. People frequently lose coordination of mind and body once they start to move physically. One common cause of this loss is movements that aren't fully natural and relaxed. Make sure that while you're trying to release tension in one part of the body, you're not creating tension in another body part by means of a stiff, awkward action. To fully understand this will require actually examining yourself, your posture, your movements, and others' movements as well. What's a natural and relaxed movement?

The rubbing, tapping, and massaging actions described above are fairly ordinary, but the transmission of ki (yuki) requires more explanation. Once more, if you center yourself in the hara and relax, it's possible to unify the mind and body. It is only in this state of mind-body harmony that you can effectively project ki. Visualization is the most basic way for beginners to enhance projection of ki in the above healing arts. To this end, first gently touch the area you'll be treating. Next, focus on the projection of ki into the body for sev- eral seconds, and follow this by gradually apply- ing pressure in the direc- tion of the ki flow until the

It isn't necessary to knead, hit, or in any way force the body to relax. The goal is to create a situation in which the body will heal itself or keep itself healthy. It's unnatural to coerce the body.

fingers feel resistance. Then, simply sustain the movement of ki and concentration for 30 seconds or more as you hold the pressure steadily.

Remember as well that tension in the fingertips, hands, or arms that are being used to transmit ki hinders its movement. In fact, ten- sion in general is problematic. If you can feel the muscles strongly in your fingers, hands, or arms during yuki, you're probably too tense. Altering your posture and way of using your hands is needed.

Unlike shiatsu finger pressure therapy, the flat part of the fingertip is not used. Rather, the ball of the fingertip is employed, which results in a more concentrated use of ki and force. This less diffused use of power gives practitioners greater effect with less effort. (It also requires that we keep our fingernails very short so as not to inadvertently engage in acupuncture!)

It's easy to end up pressing with the fingertips in a way that isn't conducive to a direct penetration of ki. Make sure you use the center of the fingertip as illustrated in Figure 51. If you feel the pressure on your fingertip slipping up, down, or off to the sides, you'll have an inefficient

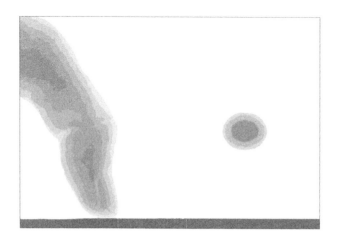

Fig. 51. When you press with your fingers, always be sure to use the center of the fingertip.

transference of energy. Notice the sensation at the fingertips when you treat yourself. It can change from moment to moment, and the angle of force needs to be correct.

Don't let your mind get stuck on where you're touching. Ki should continue to flow into the body endlessly. Mental attachment stops this flow, and ongoing concentration without attachment is essential. (As in anjo daza ho, ki is directed toward the body or the sound of a bell, but it doesn't become stuck on it. This is the rationale behind using a fading note as opposed to a constant sound.)

It isn't necessary to knead, hit, or in any way force the body to relax. The goal is to create a situation in which the body will heal itself or keep itself healthy. It's unnatural to coerce the body. If you apply the above techniques yet still feel muscle stiffness (for instance), don't necessarily use more force. Simply stay in that spot longer or increase the number of repetitions.

Spending extra time on areas that seem to be weak or stiff makes sense. Trying to force a response is actually dangerous. Likewise, instead of doing a great deal of hitori ryoho infrequently, you'll be better off engaging in a modest amount of practice on a regular basis. To see the benefits of these healing arts, it's necessary to practice regularly, spending extra time on areas with weak ki. Over a period of weeks, the benefits gradually become apparent, although hitori ryoho is relaxing and pleasant from day one.

As a side note, Nakamura Tempu Sensei was a medical doctor. Unlike some practitioners of Asian holistic health methods, he didn't feel any sense of competition with mainstream Western medicine. It was his opinion that Shin-shin-toitsu-do and Western medicine should work hand in hand. Along these lines, make a point of getting regular check-ups from your physician, and if you're ill or injured, or if you suspect that you might have a problem with your body, consult with your doctor. It is, at the very least, essential to find out what your options are.

You can quickly review these important points by using the list at the beginning of this chapter. Don't just memorize the words—find out for yourself what they actually mean.

YASASHII: "gentle kindness," painted in the sosho, or abstract and cursive, style of the monk Chiei. In Shin-shin-toitsu-do, we find good health in a gentle, relaxed, and flexible body. Realizing our innate unity with the universe in Shin-shin-toitsu-do meditation, we treat all creations with compassion. And in exercises like orenai te, we manifest an exceptional power. Yet it is a power based on unity instead of contention, and it expresses itself through gentle kindness.

Chapter 9

SIMPLE STRETCHING EXERCISES FOR HEALTH

FIVE PRINCIPLES FOR JUNAN TAISO

1. Gradually increase your range of flexibility.

2. Relax and avoid forcing your body to stretch.

3. Follow the natural sequence of movements.

4. Maintain a natural, consistent rhythm that promotes mind and body unification.

5. Put ki into each movement.

A wide variety of moving and stretching exercises are found in Japanese yoga. The following *suwari taiso*, or "sitting exercises," are included in some (but not all) versions of Shin-shin-toitsu-do. They appear to be a derivative of Makko Ho exercises, which were developed and popularized by Nagai Haruka Sensei and his father. These taiso come under the general category of *junan taiso*, in which *junan* means "flexible." Using stretching exercises as a means of cultivating flexibility, health, and longevity is something that's received a fair amount of media attention in recent years, and the value of yogic stretching and similar methods is now widely recognized. Through such techniques it's possible to promote health in a broad variety of ways, including deeper relaxation, better blood circulation, and enhanced flexibility.

While most of us probably know the purpose and rationale of such exercises, the following selection from the time-honored *Tao Te Ching* briefly summarizes the theory behind stretching for health:

> A man is born gentle and weak.
> At his death he is hard and stiff.
> Green plants are tender and filled with sap.
> At their death they are withered and dry.
>
> Therefore the stiff and unbending is the disciple of death.
> The gentle and yielding is the disciple of life.
>
> Thus an army without flexibility never wins a battle.
> A tree that is unbending is easily broken.
>
> The hard and strong will fall.
> The soft and weak will overcome.[6]

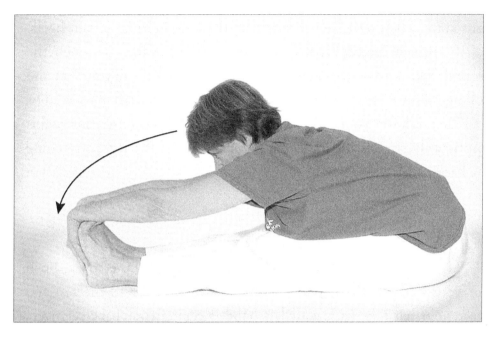

Fig. 52. Forward Stretch. Sit with the legs outstretched and reach toward your toes with a gentle, four-beat rhythm.

1. Forward Stretch

Sit with the legs outstretched. Curl your toes back and push out your heels so that your feet bend back at a 70-degree angle. Keep the knees straight. Curling the toes back stretches the muscles on the underside of the legs and helps maintain straight knees during the stretch.

Sit with your back fairly erect (at a 90-degree angle to the floor) with your arms parallel to the ground and your fingers pointing toward your toes. Then, thinking of your hara as an imaginary hinge, bend forward from this point, and reach toward your toes with a gentle, four-beat rhythm (Figure 52). Literally inch your way forward, directing

217

your ki to a point over your toes and on the floor in front of your heels.

Eventually, you'll be able to reach over your toes to touch the ground. You can also try grasping your toes or the balls of your feet and pulling calmly with both arms to help you stretch forward more readily.

Do not lower your head to your knees. In this exercise your goal is to primarily stretch the feet, ankles, and backs of the legs. Stretching the back deeply will come next.

2. Spread-Leg Stretch

Open your legs as widely as possible. Curl your toes back, push out your heels, and straighten your legs. Reach over to the left and grasp your left toes with your left hand. Keeping your back relatively straight, swing the fingertips of your right arm over toward your left foot as well and lean to the left. Using light, rhythmic movements while pulling with your left hand, gradually work your head down to your left knee. Then, repeat the same procedure to the right and, using your hands, open your legs a bit wider. Take a look at Figure 53 to see this exercise. We usually stretch one more time to the left and then to the right. This is followed by using the hands to open the legs even wider since we've just loosened the muscles in the legs, hips, and side of the torso, making this opening possible. The wider you open your legs, with a 160-degree angle as your goal, the easier it is to perform the next part of exercise 2.

Now, place your fists at arm's length, one on top of the other, on the floor in front of you. Bending from your hara while rotating your pelvis forward and down, lean forward and work your head down to touch your fists using a gentle, rocking motion. Repeat the same proce-

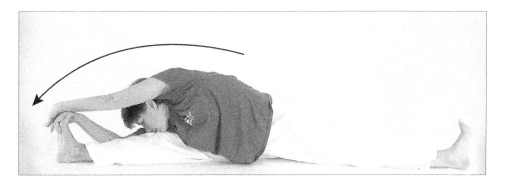

Fig. 53. Spread-Leg Stretch. Open your legs wide. Using light, rhythmic movements, gradually work your head down to your knee. Then repeat on the other side, with your legs open a bit wider. Stretch one more time to the left and then to the right. Open the legs even wider; a 160-degree angle is your goal.

Fig. 54. Place your fists on the floor in front of you, one on top of the other, at arm's length. Bend from your hara, lean forward, and work your head down to touch your fists. Repeat, but this time bring your head to the height of one fist. Finally, touch your head, and if possible your chest, to the ground.

dure, but this time bring your head to only one fist. Finally, touch your head, and if possible your chest, to the ground as in Figure 54. You can also try grasping a stable object in front of you. Using this handhold, you can gently pull yourself forward. Your objective is to stretch your legs, hips, groin area, and back.

Fig. 55. Seated Stretch. Bring both feet together in front of your groin. Grip your toes and feet with both hands. Tap against the ground by raising and dropping both knees rhythmically.

3. Seated Stretch

Bring the soles of both feet together in front of your groin. Ideally, your heels should be about one fist width from your body and in line with your knees. Grip your toes and feet with both hands, and keep your back erect at a 90-degree angle to the ground with your shoulders down.

Next, tap your knees against the ground by raising and dropping both knees rhythmically (Figure 55). Relax completely and move naturally. As flexibility increases, your knees will be able to strike the ground easily. Do not force them.

Now that you've loosened the hip and groin areas, bend from the

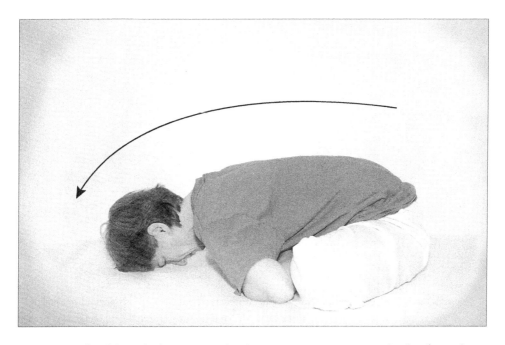

Fig. 56. Next, bend from the hara, using a four-beat motion as you aim your head in front of your feet on the floor. Pull with both hands to get more leverage.

hara, keeping your back fairly straight, and aim your head toward a spot in front of your feet on the floor (Figure 56). Use a gentle, four-beat, rhythmic motion as you gradually work your way down. Since you're holding your toes, you can pull with both hands to get a bit more leverage to go farther.

Exercise three stretches the hips, groin, and legs. The back is also stretched, even down into the sacral/tailbone area—something that wasn't accomplished in the first two exercises. Exercise two stretches the groin area, while the third exercise provides a deeper stretch for these muscles. One exercise leads into another, and the order of these stretches is important.

Fig. 57. Seiza Twist Stretch. Sit lightly on your heels in seiza. Swing your arms around to the left, and when you've gone as far as you can, place your left hand on the ground. Then, work your head to the floor between your hands, using a steady, rocking motion. Your right hand will also come into contact with the ground. Repeat to the right side.

4. Seiza Twist Stretch

Now kneel and sit lightly on your heels in the seiza position. Swing your arms in a large circle to the rear as if you were drawing an arc with your fingertips. Swing to the left, and when you've gone as far as comfortably possible, place your left hand on the ground. Then, progressively work your head to the floor between your hands using a steady, four-beat, rocking motion. As your head moves downward, your right hand will also come into contact with the ground as in Figure 57. Repeat this twisting action to the right as well.

Thus far we've explored exercises that involve bending to the front and side. Exercise four is the first twisting motion. Sitting in seiza itself

Fig. 58. Seiza Back Stretch. From seiza, ease yourself onto your back, keeping your feet tucked under your hips. Interlace your fingers, turn your palms over, and stretch up and away from your head. Raise your right shoulder off the ground and twist to the left. Then twist to the right. Continue to roll over your shoulders and from side to side.

produces a gentle stretch of the legs, knees, and ankles. Twisting flexes the back and aligns the spine. When you twist to the left, as your head nears the floor you'll also feel a stretch in your left arm, left side of your chest, and left shoulder.

5. Seiza Back Stretch

Next, while still sitting in seiza, use your hands and forearms to slowly ease yourself onto your back. Your feet remain tucked under your hips. Interlace your fingers, turning the palms over, and stretch up and away from your head as in the last form of hitori ryoho. This should look like Figure 58. Then, raise your right shoulder off the

SIMPLE STRETCHING EXERCISES FOR HEALTH

ground, and twist to the left. Follow this by raising the left shoulder and twisting to the right. Continue to roll back and forth over your shoulders and from side to side. (This insures that both sides of the abdominal area and intestines are affected.) As you do so, keep your knees close together and down on the ground while you also keep both arms fully extended.

This exercise stretches the thighs, knees, ankles, back, abdominal area, chest, shoulders, arms, wrists, and fingers. If you feel excessive pain in your knees, placing a folded towel, blanket, or cushion between your buttocks and legs can sometimes help. Similarly, placing a folded towel between your ankles and the floor can ease ankle pain. And if you cannot lean all the way back, try piling up a number of pillows. Then, over a period of weeks, gradually remove one pillow at a time, thus easing yourself downward. By using your imagination, you can find other props to help yourself perform these exercises.

We should be relaxed enough within movement that we can breathe more or less as we would at any other time, even though we're practicing stretching exercises. This is one of the fundamental indicators of true relaxation in action—even as we move or perform a given action, the breathing pattern remains undisturbed.

6. Rolling Exercise

Sit with your legs crossed and the small of your back straight. Place your left foot in front of your right, which is tucked in toward your hips. Leave a space of about 8 inches between your feet. Allow your chest to open, drop your shoulders, and look to the horizon. Rest your

Fig. 59. Rolling Exercise. Sit with your legs crossed, one foot in front of the other, which is tucked in toward your hips. Open your chest, drop your shoulders, and look to the horizon. Rest your hands lightly on top of your feet and lean slightly forward.

hands lightly on top of your feet. Lean forward a bit so that you feel your weight shift toward the underside of your knees, as well as forward and down toward your lower abdomen (Figure 59).

Next, pushing off the ground softly with your feet, tuck your chin to your chest, round your back, and gently roll backward. Every part of your back, especially your lower back, touches the floor as you roll. Be careful not to let your head hit the ground. To prevent this, keep the chin tucked in and stop rolling when your feet are pointing straight up at the ceiling. Relax your legs as you roll, letting them respond to centrifugal force, and allow your legs to straighten out as you roll back. Your hands slide from your feet to lightly touch the tops of your knees

Fig. 60. Next, push off with your feet; tuck your chin, round your back, and gently roll backward. Relax and allow the legs to straighten as you roll, and stop rolling when your feet are pointing at the ceiling. Now roll forward, bringing your chin away from your chest and looking straight ahead. Uncurl your back and let your hands slide back to your feet. As you finish, lean forward slightly but keep an erect posture. Repeat, and switch your feet in the air each time.

as well. This keeps your legs from going too far back over your head (Figure 60).

As you roll back to the front, bringing your chin away from your chest, look straight ahead. Simultaneously start to uncurl your back and let your hands slide back down to their original position touching your feet. You end up leaning forward slightly with an erect posture that's identical to your starting position—with one exception.

Just before you roll back to your original position, switch your legs in mid-air so that when your feet touch the ground, your right foot is now in front. The goal is to massage your back by rolling along the surface of the floor. This massage will relax and soften the muscles on either side of the spine. When your right leg is tucked in closest to your body, lean a bit to the right as you roll back along the muscles near the right side of the spine. Then, switch your feet in the air just before your roll forward so that when you come to a stop, your left leg is tucked in closest to your body. As you roll back again, you incline to the left side, alternating legs and sides of the backbone as you rock back and forth rhythmically.

As you roll forward, focus your ki forward through whatever is in front of you, letting it carry on endlessly even after your body has stopped moving. This mental image makes it easier to rock back to your starting position, and it promotes coordination of mind and body.

Important Points

Stretching methods are usually done in one of two ways. We can either slowly stretch the body as far as it will go and then hold this position, or we can bounce up and down, using a fairly large motion. The latter has a greater tendency to cause sore muscles and injuries. However, the above exercises don't use either common approach, and instead feature a small, gentle, rocking motion.

Extend one arm, stiffen it, and hold it in place. It should be fairly easy to maintain the tension. Now, extend your arm again and shake your fingertips and arm. While you continue to shake, try to stiffen and lock the muscles in your arm. After trying this once or twice, it's clear

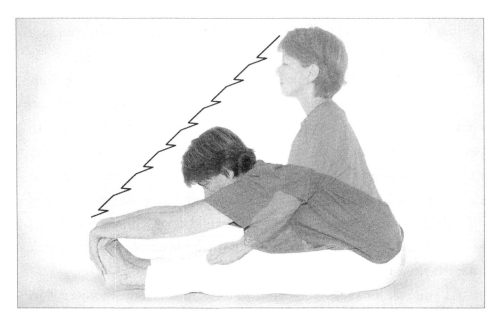

Fig. 61. When stretching, aim for a small, advancing, incremental movement in a four-beat rhythm. Each movement travels a bit farther than the one before.

that it's easier to keep your muscles stiff when your arm is held in place than when its moving, because to sustain movement, your muscles cannot lock up in a tense manner. This is the rationale behind using a gentle, progressive rocking motion as you work your way down to the ground in exercises one, two, three, and four. Think of this as a small, advancing, incremental type of movement. It's done to a four-beat rhythm. Each time you move, try to go a bit farther than the time before, as in Figure 61. Don't move, return to your original position, and then move again. Make a slow, gradual, and continuous progression.

You must pay close attention to where you are and what you're doing. As a result, this relatively small, incremental, and progressive movement guarantees that you keep your mind in the moment. Since a constant forward progression is involved, we're encouraged to sustain a continuous forward projection of ki as well. Using a calm, steady four-beat rhythm as we rock back and forth on the way to completing the stretch helps to calm the mind and relax the body. And all of this amounts to coordination of mind and body in action.

In addition, don't try to become flexible overnight. You'll only strain or injure your muscles, which is a definite setback on the path to greater limberness. Likewise, your initial movements within each exercise should be done softly, gradually stretching farther as you go. This allows your muscles to warm up before they're flexed more deeply.

Relaxation is essential for pliability, and a natural rhythm can be an aid to relaxation. Once again, keep a steady, calm rhythm to promote a calmer state of mind and body. Aim for one beat per second. You can count slowly to yourself as you work your way down to the ground. If you have relaxing music that features a four-beat rhythm, you can perform these exercises to the music. Explore the relationship between rhythm, relaxation, and coordination, as this is one of the central tenets of Shin-shin-toitsu-do.

You can also try exhaling as you lean toward earth, which is a simple of way of aiding relaxation. Eventually we should be relaxed enough within movement that we can breathe more or less as we would at any other time, even though we're practicing stretching exercises. This is one of the fundamental indicators of true relaxation in action—even as we move or perform a given action, the breathing pattern remains undisturbed.

Note as well the order in which these exercises are performed. Each movement prepares the body for the subsequent action. Changing the order results in less efficiency; although it's possible after running through the series one time to go back and work on specific exercises that you're having trouble with.

These exercises are commonly performed with the aid of a partner who holds or presses on various parts of your body, making it easier to stretch. The inclusion of such *hodo taiso*, or "assisted exercises," is beyond the scope of this volume.

Rhythm isn't only useful for promoting relaxation in action and coordinated movement, it's also an indicator of mind and body unification. Whenever the mind becomes attached to a thought, feeling, or external object, the movement of ki is inhibited, and rhythm tends to break.

To help maintain rhythm, a constant projection of ki, and the unity of mind and body, refer back to Experiment One in Chapter 2. In this experiment, we studied how to bring the fingertips together effortlessly via the movement of the mind and ki. Just as you willed your fingertips together in this experiment, you can mentally direct your head to the floor in, for example, the spread-leg stretch. Experiment with using your mind to move your body in stretching. This doesn't mean that your muscles aren't to be used, but instead, that you should study the effectiveness of using mental movement to aid your muscles in accomplishing a given task. When you get the hang of it, you'll find that you're stretching by the unification of progressive relaxation, rhythm, and concentration more than by straining.

And this is as it should be. Because in the end, what we're really studying in Japanese yoga—even more than how to stretch—is Shin-shin-toitsu-do, "the Way of mind and body unification."

AFTERWORD

Shin-shin-toitsu-do is an art of mind and body unification. Since the mind controls the body, it's common to guide the mind to facilitate this coordination. The positive use of the mind and concentration are central to this experience. Some might think that the essence of this Way lies in controlling ourselves. Paradoxically, the easiest way to "control" yourself is to not focus on the self. The more comfortable and relaxed we are, the less self-conscious we are, and vice versa.

We've all experienced self-consciousness as shyness, embarrassment, self-doubt, or some related condition, and we can recognize the amount of discomfort associated with this state. What we often fail to grasp is that we're frequently trapped by self-consciousness on a regular basis, but it's only when we're under stress or when we've made a mistake (or fear making one) that we come face-to-face with our self-consciousness. We uncover, in other words, what's already there.

In studying Japanese brush writing, for instance, beginners must learn to hold the brush in an unfamiliar way and move it to create unfamiliar characters. Frequently, they focus their attention on the fingers gripping the brush and hold it tightly to try to control it and themselves. This rarely works. Actually, once the basic grip has been understood, the fastest way to progress is to forget it and focus on the paper where the characters will soon appear. Stopping the mind at the brush, in an attempt to control the hand, the brush, and the self, only stops the movement of ki and makes control impossible. The other approach allows ki to be transmitted into the work, and the brush and painted characters correctly follow the ki movement. (Like the self, you don't so much "control" ki as harmonize with it.)

In Japanese calligraphy, the more we think of controlling ourselves, the less we're capable of concentrating on the paper and the task at hand. But this isn't limited to the Way of calligraphy.

A similar truth can be seen in *kenjutsu* ("the art of the sword"), *jojutsu* ("the art of the 4-foot staff"), and related Japanese martial arts. The more we focus on trying to hold the weapon tightly, trapping the mind and ki where we grasp it, the less we can control the actual path of the blade or staff. To make a sword move in a certain direction and stop at a specific spot, the mind must lead it in that direction—the mind must move outwardly. But when attempting to consciously control the self and weapon, the mind is on the self. It isn't leading the weapon, and thus no mind and body coordination takes place.

Some teachers of Shin-shin-toitsu-do have emphasized that the essence of mind and body unification lies in focusing the mind quickly and positively on an action, relaxing, then following through physically without the slightest hesitation. Concentrating over and over before acting not only betrays a lack of actual confidence but also subconsciously encourages it. (If we can *really* perform effectively, why would we have to tell ourselves over and over that this is the case?)

Similarly, hesitation means a gap between the mind that moves and the body that reacts. We hesitate because we're afraid of failure, which is yet another expression of self-consciousness. Therefore, we can sum up coordination of mind and body by stating that:

The mind should focus quickly and positively, and the relaxed body should follow through without hesitation or further deliberation.

This is most easily achieved when we concentrate the mind deeply on what needs to be done, and then leave the results up to the universe.

These two points are very simple as well as powerful, and I hope we can use this book as a catalyst to explore their genuine meaning in the course of our daily lives. But trying to use these points to unify the mind and body isn't enough. They're really quite simple, clear, and easy to understand. So why are we commonly unable to utilize them in a practical way and on a regular basis in everyday life? This question is equally important to examine, and the answer lies in the mind's attachment to the concept of the self. It's the self's fear of failure and its related desires and attachments that causes us to hesitate—the same self that experiences anxiety over results. Experiment with the coordination of mind and body and personally discover if this is actually the case. Merely reading my statements, written from my perspective, is absolutely not equivalent to what must be seen and done firsthand.

Self-consciousness, then, is a problem that's not limited to a particular activity, but is rather a condition that many of us exist in, and which manifests itself to undermine our freedom of expression. To deal with this, we must look into the actual nature of the self. When we think of our "self," what are we considering? Is this the real self? Can it be damaged or destroyed? Does it exist as something separate from the universe? And if it's not separate, can it be controlled? Why do we want to control it? All of this must be considered or the examination of self-consciousness will be too superficial to have any real impact.

How attachments relate to self-consciousness is another vital consideration. We hesitate, we grip the brush too tightly, and we try to control the self, to get something we want or to avoid failure. None of this works well, and it actually increases the likelihood of failing. Attachment relates to all of this, and the self is tied into attachment.

In short, while it's possible to increase our health and personal effectiveness tremendously by practicing Japanese yoga, there will be events in life that are simply beyond our control. To paraphrase an oft-quoted saying, we should change what we can, accept what we can't change, and be able to tell the difference between the two. This is really just common sense and pretty hard to dispute. So why don't we do it?

Even though Shin-shin-toitsu-do gives us a powerful tool for human transformation, if it's mistakenly used to further an illusion of total control, self-consciousness, and attachment, it only continues to perpetuate fear. Although it may give us a feeling of power, which in turn may create a sense of confidence and composure, it will not eradicate fear if approached in the wrong way. It will cover up fear, only to have this fear continue to resurface. (This is similar to the manner in which a drug can momentarily give us a feeling of calmness or power, but the underlying problems of existence remain.)

Clearly we try to control even what's beyond our control out of fear. Fear ties in, again, to the self and attachment. While all of the above topics have been explored in various ways throughout this text, I felt it was important to re-emphasize and summarize them at the conclusion of this book. If you genuinely consider these comments, you'll quickly realize that they denote not a conclusion but a jumping off point . . . a leap into the unknown.

SOURCES FOR INSTRUCTION & SUPPLIES

In Shin-shin-toitsu-do, at least half of practice is conducted with other people's help. As you read this book, I'm sure it became clear that you'd need to work with a partner to try some aspects of Japanese yoga.

Moreover, our practice of these exercises must be practical and aimed at everyday life. Sitting completely still, alone in a silent room, with eyes closed, is relaxing and fine for seated meditation. And while it's worthwhile to practice under such conditions, daily living for most of us is rather far removed from such an environment. To discover unification of mind and body in ordinary life, Shin-shin-toitsu-do practice emphasizes meditation in motion, learning to coordinate mind and body with eyes open, and practice with others. In many ways, the easiest way to harmonize the mind and body is to sit still while alone. Coordination of mind and body in motion is harder, and maintaining this state of unification in action and in relationship to others is even more difficult. And the latter represents most closely almost everyone's daily life.

Ongoing Practice

If you'd like to find people to practice with or find out more about what we're studying at the Sennin Foundation Center for Japanese Cultural Arts, you can write or send e-mail to:

The Sennin Foundation Center
for Japanese Cultural Arts
1053 San Pablo Avenue
Albany, CA 94706 USA
Website: www.senninfoundation.com
Email: hedavey@aol.com

In addition, the Sennin Foundation, Inc., sponsors a free Internet web site called Michi Online that regularly features authentic information about various classical Japanese arts as well as Shin-shin-toitsu-do. To take a look at Michi Online and check out the latest issue of the *Michi Online Journal of Japanese Cultural Arts*, just go to:

www.michionline.org

For people who can read Japanese, it's possible to consult Nakamura Tempu Sensei's own writings, some of which are listed in the notes section, below. They contain information about his teachings and the organization that he left behind.

Buying Meditation Bells

To practice anjo daza ho, you'll need a Japanese meditation bell. This is the metal, bowl-shaped bell mentioned in Chapter 6. Hitting the edge of the bell with its wooden striker creates a mellow, lengthy, resonant tone. Try to purchase a larger bell of top-quality metal that will sustain its tone for a longer period.

Most Buddhist supply stores stock such a bell, and you can also contact a local Buddhist church or Asian gift store to see if they can help you buy one. If you can't find one, try the following shop:

Soko Hardware
1698 Post Street
San Francisco, CA 94115
Telephone: 415-931-5510

NOTES

1. Mary Lutyens, *Krishnamurti: His Life and Death* (New York: St. Martins Press, 1990), p. 75.

2. Eddie Lau, "Intuition's Real? Experiments Try to Prove It," *Sacramento Bee* (October 20, 1999), p. B4.

3. Nakamura Tempu and Hashimoto Tetsuichi, *"Ways for Unification of Mind and Body"* (Tokyo: self-published, n.d.), p. 2.

4. Howard Kent, *Yoga Made Easy* (Allentown, Pennsylvania: People's Medical Society, 1993), p. 90.

5. Nakamura and Hashimoto, *"Ways for Unification of Mind and Body,"* p. 2.

6. Lao Tsu, *Tao Te Ching*, trans. Gia-fu Feng and Jane English (New York: Vintage Books, 1972), p. 155.

This is the first book in English that concentrates on Nakamura Tempu Sensei and his system of Japanese yoga. During my research I found the following books on ki especially useful and informative:

Reed, William. *A Road That Anyone Can Walk: Ki*. Tokyo and New York: Japan Publications, 1992.

Tohei, Koichi. *Ki in Daily Life*. Revised edition. Tochigi, Japan: Ki no Kenkyukai H.Q., 2001.

I also made use of the following works in Japanese, listed here by title and author. These books are privately published or are made available by the Tempu-kai.

Anjo Daza Kosho (Igaku Kara Mita Toitsu-do), by Nakamura Tempu.

Kenko to Kofuku e no Michi, Yasutake Sadao.

Kenshin Sho, Nakamura Tempu.

Kyukyoku no Makko-Ho, Kamo Masumi.

Makko-Ho Hodo Taiso, Makko-Ho Kyokai.

Renshin Sho, Nakamura Tempu.

Seiko no Jitsugen, Nakamura Tempu.

Shinjinsei no Tankyu, Nakamura Tempu.

Shinri Gyoshu Shokushu, Nakamura Tempu.

Tempu Sensei Zadan, Uno Chiyo.

Uchu no Hibiki: Nakamura Tempu no Sekai, Kamiwatari Ryoei.

GLOSSARY

agura: sitting with the legs crossed

aikido: "the Way to union with ki," a Japanese martial Way

aiki-jujutsu: a traditional Japanese martial art

anjo daza ho: Shin-shin-toitsu-do meditation on the fading tone of a bell

asana: the physical postures used in classical Indian Hatha yoga

batto-jutsu: a form of Japanese swordsmanship

budo: the martial Way

bushi: a Japanese warrior or samurai who followed the tenets of budo

dantei anji: "concluding suggestion," used in jiko anji

Do: "the Way"

dojo: "place of the Way," a training hall used in certain Japanese cultural and meditative arts

Dokyo: "teachings of the Way," Japanese Taoism

fudoshin: "immovable mind," a state of complete mental and physical stability

gyoga shite suru yodo ho: reclining yodo ho

hanka fuza: sitting in half-lotus position

hanpuku anji: "repeating suggestion," used in jiko anji

hara: literally, "abdomen," but used in Shin-shin-toitsu-do and other Japanese Ways to refer to the body's natural center in the lower abdomen

Hatha yoga: one of the classical forms of Indian yoga emphasizing stretching through the use of yogic postures and breathing exercises

hitori ryoho: self-healing arts

hsien: a Chinese Taoist sage or mystic

in: a hand gesture used in Shin-shin-toitsu-do and other meditation Ways, usually symbolic in nature

jiko anji: autosuggestion

judo: "the Way of gentleness and yielding," a Japanese martial sport

junan taiso: flexibility exercises

kado: the Way of flowers; Japanese flower arrangement

kekka fuza: sitting in full lotus position

ki: life energy

ki ga nukeru: the withdrawal of ki

ki no dashikata: the projection of life energy

kokoro: also pronounced *shin*; refers to the words "mind," "heart," and "spirit"

kumbhaka: an Indian term indicating the retention of breath; also used in Shin-shin-toitsu-do to indicate a particular postural state and/or breathing exercise

meirei anji: "commanding suggestion," used in jiko anji

muga ichi-nen: "no self, one thought"

muga ichi-nen ho: Shin-shin-toitsu-do meditation involving concentration on an external object, e.g., a candle's flame

naka-ima: "the eternal present"

orenai te: a Shin-shin-toitsu-do exercise involving ki projection through the arm

prana: an Indian term indicating life energy, known in Japanese as ki

Pranayama: classical Indian yogic breathing exercises

Raja yoga: one of the classical forms of Indian yoga emphasizing meditation

seiza: "correct sitting," kneeling with the legs folded under the hips while resting lightly on the heels

sennin: Japanese mountain-dwelling Taoist mystics, the Japanese equivalent to a yogi

Sennin-do: the Way of the sennin, generic for Japanese versions of Chinese Taoist yoga

Sennin Ryoji: sennin healing arts, generic for Japanese versions of Chinese Taoist healing methods

sensei: "born before," a teacher

shagande suru yodo ho: squatting yodo ho

shin-shin-toitsu: "mind and body unification"

Shin-shin-toitsu-do: "the Way of mind and body unification"

Shin-shin-toitsu-ho: also Shin-shin-toitsu-do, "the art or methods of mind and body unification"

Shin-shin-toitsu no Yondai Gensoku: "Four Basic Principles to Unify Mind and Body"

Shinto: the Way of the gods, the native Japanese religion

shodo: the Way of calligraphy

shuchu-ryoku: the power of concentration

suji: a line of muscle or nerve

suwari taiso: sitting exercises

suwatte suru yodo ho: sitting yodo ho

tanden: the lower abdomen

Taoism: native Chinese spiritual path stressing oneness with the Way of the universe

tate suru yodo ho: standing yodo ho

Toitsu-do: "the Way of unification"; same as Shin-shin-toitsu-do

uchu-rei: universal mind or spirit

wa: harmony

yodo ho: a Shin-shin-toitsu-do health exercise and meditation practice using rhythmic movement

yoga: an art, originating in India, for achieving union with the universe

yogi: a practitioner of Indian yoga

yuki: transfusion of ki; a healing method

Zen: a form of Japanese Buddhist meditation

About the Author

H. E. Davey is the Director of the Sennin Foundation Center for Japanese Cultural Arts, which offers instruction in Japanese yoga, martial arts, healing arts, and fine arts. The Sennin Foundation Center was established in the San Francisco Bay Area in 1981.

H. E. Davey's introduction to the arts of Japan came via traditional Japanese martial arts. Since the age of five, he has studied jujutsu in the U.S. and Japan. He has received the title of Kyoshi (equal to sixth- to eighth-degree black belt) from the Kokusai Budoin, a Tokyo-based international federation.

In middle school, Mr. Davey began the study of Shin-shin-toitsu-do, a Japanese yoga founded by Nakamura Tempu Sensei. He is a member of Tempu-kai and has practiced in Japan and the U.S.A. under Nakamura Sensei's senior disciples, including Hashimoto Tetsuichi Sensei. Mr. Davey has received instruction in Nakamura Sensei's methods of healing with ki and bodywork, which he also teaches. He has received instruction in Hatha yoga and Pranayama in the tradition of Ms. Indra Devi as well.

Mr. Davey has studied shodo (traditional Japanese calligraphy) directly under the late Kobara Ranseki Sensei, a recipient of the prestigious Order of the Rising Sun. Mr. Davey holds the highest rank in Ranseki Sho Juku shodo and exhibits annually in Japan.

H. E. Davey's writings and Japanese calligraphy have appeared in various American and Japanese magazines and newspapers. He is the author of *Unlocking the Secrets of Aiki-jujutsu* (McGraw-Hill) and *Brush Meditation: A Japanese Way to Mind & Body Harmony* (Stone Bridge Press), and is co-author (with Ann Kameoka) of *The Japanese Way of the Flower: Ikebana as Moving Meditation* (Stone Bridge Press).

Made in United States
North Haven, CT
26 May 2025

69218062R00135